ᴄᴏᴏᴏᴏ

MIRACLES
FROM
HEAVEN

ᴄᴏᴏᴏᴏ

Barbara Duffey

Barbara Duffey

Elysian Publishing Company
Eatonton, Georgia

Published By:

Elysian Publishing Company
113 Cherry Point
Eatonton, Georgia 31024
706-485-0741

First Printing November 1998.

Web Site: http://www.ghoststories.com

Cover design by Mary Ann May.

Cover photograph was taken by Nick Thompson. When he snapped a
picture of a cloud formation at Conyers, Georgia, this image appeared when
the photograph was instantly developed. Some people see the Virgin Mary;
others see a face which might be Jesus. This photograph was used by
special permission only and is not the property of the Elysian Publishing
Company.

Library of Congress Cataloging-in-Publication Data:

Duffey, Barbara 1943-

    Miracles from Heaven/Barbara Duffey

    Includes bibliographical references.
    ISBN 0-9659477-1-8 (pbk.)

    1. Miracles. 2. Heaven. 3. Jesus. 4. Virgin Mary.
    5. Conyers, Georgia. 6. Fatima, Portugal. 7. Lourdes, France.
    8. Medjugorje, Yugoslavia. I. Title.

CIP: 98-93557

Dedication

I dedicate this book to Harvey West
and the power of the Holy Spirit.

Table of Contents

Acknowledgements vii

Foreword.. viii

The Three Greatest Miracles of the Twentieth Century

Miracles at Fatima 1

Miracles at Medjugorje.. 36

Miracles at Conyers 52

Personal Healings at Conyers 61

The Last Visit... 78

Personal Miracle Stories

The Mysterious Brick Wall 84

Miracle at Oconee River 86

The Marble Angel 88

Amazing Aunt Grace 89

The Virgin Mary 91

A Grandfather's Approval 93

Pushed by an Angel 95

Saved From Night Terrors 97

Red Veronica 99

A Gift of Life 101

Peggy's Dream 104

A Simple Prayer 106

Out of the Darkness Came the Dawn 109

The Healing Power of Faith 113

The Death Angel 115

A Community of Love 116

A Lay Renewal Mission Trip 118

The Greatest Gift 121

Crossing the River with Jesus 124

Strawberry Daiquiris 128

Musical Serenade 131

An Angel Near Death 133

The Miracles at Lourdes 140

Personal Gifts from the Holy Spirit 156

Acknowledgements

I would like to take this time to thank all the generous people who have given their miracle stories to this collection so that others might in some way be inspired. Without their support this book would not be possible.

I also wish to thank all my friends and family, especially my husband Jeff, and daughter Meghan, whose tireless patience and help have inspired me and enabled me to complete this work.

Many others have also contributed their expertise, especially Judy Vickers, who worked patiently with me on editing the finished manuscript. Deana Burgess has become a professional at reading the final draft.

Without the generosity of all these people and the inspiration from the Holy Spirit this book could not have been written. Thank you every one.

Foreword

The Holy Spirit has plagued me for over ten years, maybe even longer. I never understood the meaning of the Holy Spirit or how it would affect my life until it took hold of me in 1987 and never let go. My books *Banshees, Bugles and Belles: True Ghost Stories of Georgia* and *Angels and Apparitions: True Ghost Stories from the South* have been about the supernatural, ghosts, angels and life after death. Writing these books was also a spiritual journey for me and an experience of discovery. Many of the stories were quite surprising to me. People who have read my first books have asked me about *Miracles from Heaven*. Are there going to be stories of apparitions and the supernatural? We love those stories.

I tell my readers, "Yes, this book is more of the same, only bigger and better than you ever dreamed.— Hang on to your hat. It's gonna be a bumpy roller coaster ride."

I view this book as the third in a secular trilogy of the discovery of supernatural phenomena and how our lives are affected by them every day. All these stories are intricately tied together. Spirits are signs to us that there is life after death. Our soul doesn't die with our body; it goes on to another realm. The appearance of the spirits of our loved ones after they die is a precious sign given to us for comfort, and peace from and by the Holy Spirit. "Blessed are they that mourn; for they shall be comforted." (Matthew 5:4)

The Holy Spirit is the Spirit of God manifested in supernatural ways. He is present in all religions and faiths. He is the most powerful supernatural force in the universe. God's Holy Spirit has dominion over both good and evil, devils and angels, the sun, moon and stars. He is here with us in small everyday situations and in the major catastrophes of the world.

"So shall it be at the end of the age; the angels shall come forth and separate the wicked from among the righteous,

"And shall cast them into the furnace of fire; there shall be wailing and gnashing of teeth." (Matthew 13:49-50)

The Holy Spirit is omnipotent, merciful, long-suffering, eternal, righteous, invisible, immutable, omnipresent, incorruptible, immortal, and all consuming. Anything is possible with the Holy Spirit.

The characters of great adventures have sought the Holy Spirit's power in many popular movies, like the struggle of good over evil and the use of "the force" in *Star Wars*, or the quest for the power of the Excalibur in *Merlin*, again a conflict of good over evil, or the search for the Ark of the Covenant and control over its power in the movie *Raiders of the Lost Ark*. The list is unending and these quests have become icons among the greats of film— even in our own hearts we wonder if these stories could be true, the answer is only seconds away. At Pentecost, Christians were given the power of the Holy Spirit. All we have to do is ask for it and believe in Jesus Christ as our Savior. For all other religions their doctrine tells them how to access that divine power.

The stories that follow are true, and in many cases the Saints didn't ask for their burdens. God chose to give his great mission of the salvation of the world to young, illiterate, poor children. For many of us, our life's work comes to us the same way. God chooses our missions for us, whether we like them or not. He sends his angels to help us complete the job. Even though sometimes we don't want to do our tasks, we know what our life's work is and why we are doing it.

I felt compelled to write this book because in many ways

it is my story. I awoke one night at 2:00 am and came downstairs to read. I was reading about the miracles at Conyers, and I reached a passage that said, "Now is the time to tell Jesus's story." These words struck me in my soul and I knew they were the answer to my question, "When should I tell my experiences about the Holy Spirit?" From that moment on everywhere I went, I received messages. Stories of miracles came to me faster than I could record them. People told me over and over again that I should tell my own story. I was reinforced on the right hand and on the left. Not many protestants understand the great Catholic miracles of Lourdes, Fatima, Medjugorje, and Conyers. Few people in my town of Milledgeville, only an hour drive from Conyers, believe that the visions Nancy Fowler saw there were true. I wrote this account so that those people can believe, so that they can have the peace that I feel.

Help came spontaneously and unexpectedly to me when I began this book, as was the case when I was looking for a picture to use on the cover. I had been pondering this question for almost a week when I was asked to sign books at a nearby book store. While I was there several people commented on the books and I mentioned my new one, *Miracles from Heaven*. I told them to go to Conyers and experience for themselves Jesus's Holy Spirit. "Miracles are happening there," I said. "Go and claim a miracle for your life."

A young man, Nick, overheard me talking about Conyers, and when the other people left, he approached me saying, "I have been to Conyers."

I was so thrilled to meet someone who had actually been there. He said that he had pictures that he took there, pictures of supernatural images, maybe the Virgin Mary. I couldn't believe my ears. This was beyond my wildest dreams of using a supernatural image from Conyers on the cover. Later, I met Nick's mother, and they gave me permission to use all his pictures in the book. This was truly a gift from God and a direct answer to my prayers.

Throughout my life I have learned to trust in God and step out in faith. I have never been let down.

I am a cancer survivor, and even after suffering through two months of radiation and almost a year of chemotherapy, I still believe in the healing power of Jesus and the Holy Spirit. I believe that I have been healed, and when it is my time to go, He, not I, will decide.

I knew from the beginning of writing this book that Jesus would put the stories He wanted in here. The stories that have been withdrawn were in most cases not appropriate for the message that has surfaced from this collection of true miracles. The messages from the three greatest miracles of the twentieth century, Fatima, Medjugorje, and Conyers are for everyone to "Pray for peace and reconciliation in the world" for the salvation of mankind.

The
Three Greatest Miracles
of the
Twentieth Century

MAP OF FATIMA

MFH Graphics

SEPTEMBER 1917—JACINTA AND LUCIA ON A VISIT TO REIXIDA

The Miracles at Fatima
⊷◌⊷

Three young children were tending their sheep in the hills of Fatima, Portugal, on May 13, 1917, when a flash of light caught their attention. The vision of a Lady dressed all in white appeared on the treetop of a holm oak. At first the young shepherds were frightened. Francisco Marto, age 9, and his sister Jacinta, age 7, were so overcome with the beauty of the vision that they were speechless, but their cousin Lucia dos Santos, age 10, conjured up enough nerve to ask the vision who she was and what she wanted. The Lady answered their questions, said they would all go to heaven, and promised that she would come back again. She appeared on the thirteenth day of each of the following six months—ending in October—and gave to these three children prophecies about the future of the world. The last appearance of the Lady was October 13, 1917, when many miracles occurred to convince the disbelieving public that the children's sightings were indeed real and that the Lady of Fatima was a messenger from God.

The Angel's First Appearance

Visions of the Lady were not the first apparitions the children saw. In the spring of 1916, Jacinta and Francisco received permission from their family to take their sheep up into the hills to graze. They were very young children to have such a responsibility, but Lucia was experienced and was to join them with her own family's flock of sheep. So the three were granted permission to go up into the hills. A soft mist of rain fell that day, and the children sought shelter in a hollow among the rocks of an olive grove owned jointly by Lucia's uncle and several other villagers. The following quotes and excerpts have been taken from the book *Fatima in Lucia's Own Words, Sister Lucia's Memoirs.*

The children rushed through their rosary, saying only, "Hail Mary" and "Our Father" on each bead instead of the entire verse so they could quickly eat their lunch and return to their play. On this day they began Jacinta's favorite game called "pebbles" but were interrupted when a gust of wind violently shook the olive trees above them. Fearing the arrival of a sudden storm, the children gazed past the tree tops up at the sky to see what was happening. The children watched in great awe as an angel glided slowly down from the clouds toward them. As it drew closer, they were able to distinguish the fine features of a young man fourteen or fifteen years old. He was whiter than snow, transparent as crystal, and of great beauty.

The angel said to them, "Fear not. I am the Angel of Peace. Pray with me." The children immediately knelt down, touched their foreheads to the ground, following his example, and repeated this prayer three times as he directed: "O my God, I believe, I adore, I hope and I love Thee. I ask pardon for those who do not believe, do not adore, do not hope and do not love thee."

When he arose, he said, "Pray thus. The hearts of Jesus and Mary are attentive to your supplications."

Lucia reported later to the Bishop, "These words engraved themselves so deeply in our minds, that we could never forget them. We spent hours prostrate like the angel, repeating his words, until we fell to the ground exhausted. I warned my companions right away that this vision must be kept secret even from our parents."

The children didn't see another vision until the summer of 1916 when they were playing on the stone slabs of a well down at the bottom of a garden belonging to Lucia's parents. Suddenly, they saw the same angel standing beside them.

This time he said, "What are you doing? Pray! Pray a great deal. The hearts of Jesus and Mary have merciful designs on you. Offer prayers and sacrifices continually to the Most High."

"How are we to make sacrifices?" Lucia asked.

"Make of everything you can a sacrifice, and offer it to God as an act of reparation for the sins by which God is offended and as a petition for the conversion of sinners. You will thus draw down peace to your country in this way. I am the Guardian Angel of Portugal. Above all, accept and bear with submission all the suffering the Lord will send you."

This was quite a message for the children to hear, and after praying the rosary completely, they quickly ran down through the green pastures driving their sheep home, but never spoke of it until years later.

The next angel sighting wasn't until the fall of the same year. The children climbed high into the hills above Fatima with their flocks and drove their sheep over some steep, rocky slopes above the olive grove at Pregueira. After their lunch, they knelt down in a hollow of rocks with their foreheads touching the ground and began to say the prayer of the first Angel: "My God. I believe, I adore, I hope...."

They said the prayer many times before an extraordinary light suddenly shone down upon them. They sprang up to see what was happening and beheld the Angel. He was holding a golden chalice in his left hand, with the Host suspended above it, from which some drops of Blood fell into the chalice. Leaving the chalice suspended in the air, the Angel knelt down beside them and made them repeat three times:

"Most Holy Trinity, Father, Son and Holy Spirit, I offer You the most precious Body, Blood, Soul and Divinity of Jesus

Christ, present in all the tabernacles of the world, in reparation for the outrages, sacrilege and indifference with which He Himself is offended. And, through the infinite merits of His most Sacred Heart, and the Immaculate Heart of Mary, I beg of You the conversion of poor sinners."

Then, rising, he took the chalice and the Host in his hands. He gave the Sacred Host to Lucia and shared the Blood from the Chalice between Jacinta and Francisco, saying as he did so:

"Take and drink the Body and Blood of Jesus Christ, horribly outraged by ungrateful men! Make reparation for their crimes and console your God."

Once again, he prostrated himself on the ground and repeated with them, three times more, the same prayer, "Most Holy Trinity. . ." and then disappeared.

Francisco later managed to say, "The angel gave you Holy Communion, Lucia, but what was it that he gave Jacinta and me?"

"It was also Communion," Jacinto interrupted. "Didn't you see the Blood dripping from the Host?"

"I knew it was God within me," the boy admitted, "but I didn't know how it was." Then Francisco fell prostrate to the ground, praying until dark, overwhelmed with what had happened.

Later Lucia reported, "We remained a long time in this position, repeating the same words over and over again. When at last we got up, we noticed that it was already dark, and time to return home."

The three children didn't see another vision until the following year.

JACINTA, FRANCISCO, AND LUCIA

MFH Graphics

The Vision of the Lady

On Sunday, May 13, 1917, preceding the Ascension and the Feast Day of Our Lady of the Blessed Sacrament, Lucia decided to take their flocks to the Cova da Iria—a vast natural hollow of ground three kilometers away—which was owned by her family. The children ran through the meadow picking up stones to build a small shelter around a fruze bush to keep the sheep from eating it. Suddenly they saw a flash of light and looked up into the clear, blue sky. They saw nothing unusual until there was another flash of light. A Lady suddenly appeared to them, bathed in a dazzling circle of light and stood on top of a holm oak tree. The children's eyes hurt from the Lady's brilliant glow and beauty. Beams of light radiated out far enough from Her body to engulf each one of the children. The Blessed Lady looked down at them so fondly that they weren't afraid.

Lucia later described the Lady as being "more brilliant than the sun and radiating a light clearer and more intense than a crystal filled with glittering water and transpierced by the rays of the most burning sun."

"Do not be afraid," the Lady said in a gentle voice. "I will do you no harm."

"Where are you from?" Lucia asked.

"I am from Heaven."

The children described the Lady's dress as a white mantle of immaculate purity, bordered by a stronger golden light which fell to her feet. A prominent star shone from the hem of this "sun-like robe." From her hands hung a rosary of diamond-like brilliance.

"What do you want from us?" Lucia asked.

"I come to ask you to come here on the thirteenth day for six months at the same time, and then I will tell you who I am and what I want of you. And afterwards I will return here a seventh time."

Gaining confidence Lucia asked, "Will I go to heaven?"

"Yes you will."

"And Jacinta?"

"She also."

"And Francisco? Will he go to heaven too?"

The Lady paused and looked at Francisco. Then she said, "Yes. But first he must say many rosaries."

Lucia asked about the souls of two girls who recently died in Aljustrel, and the Lady replied that "one was already in heaven and the other would be in purgatory until the end of the world."

"Would you like to offer yourselves to God to accept all the sufferings which he may send you in reparation for the countless sins by which he is offended and in supplication for the conversion of sinners?"

Lucia answered for all three, "Yes, we would."

"Then you will have much to suffer, but the grace of God will be your comfort." As the Lady said these words, she opened her palms, and streams of light flowed out from her hands and penetrated the souls of the children, causing them to feel "lost in God," whom they recognized in that light. After the light ceased, the children threw themselves to the ground and cried out in unison, "O most Holy Trinity. I adore thee! My God, My God, I love Thee in The Most Blessed Sacrament!"

When they had finished, the Lady asked them to recite the rosary every day. Then she rose in a cloud of brilliant light the same way she came and disappeared into the eastern sky.

Jacinta was so excited that she kept jumping up and down saying, "Oh, what a beautiful Lady. Oh, what a beautiful Lady."

Lucia was afraid if the news of the apparition got out, no one would believe them and they would be laughed at. So she

made Francisco and Jacinto promise again not to say a word about
the apparition to anyone.

But Francisco was overcome by the experience and said,
"We were on fire in that light and yet we were not burned. How
wonderful God is. How can we ever describe Him? It would be
impossible and yet—he looked so sad. If only I could console
him."

Jacinta was so excited about seeing the vision that she
couldn't remain silent and immediately told her parents. They
were reluctant to believe her, but by the next morning all the
village had heard about the sighting. Most of the villagers didn't
believe the children's story and reprimanded them severely. Some
even spit at them for "telling their lies."

Lucia's mother, Maria Rosa, was the most angry of all the
people in the village. She couldn't believe that her daughter would
lie about seeing a Lady in the light. She had always taught Lucia
that lying was a sin. Lucia's mother beat her severely and repeatedly with a broom stick in hopes that she would admit that the
story about the "Blessed Lady" was a lie.

After Lucia's beatings, the children remembered the Holy
Lady's words that they would suffer much, and they accepted the
ridicule. They offered the offenses and abuses they received up
to Jesus for the remission of the sins and for the conversion of
sinners. Every day the children prayed the rosary as directed and
gave their lunch to the poor beggar children, offering their own
hunger as a suffering for the remission of the sins of the ungodly
and the conversion of sinners. Every day they took their flocks
up into the hills to graze just as they had always done.

On the morning of June 13, 1917, a few dozen curious
people decided to join the children when they went to the Cova
da Iria to see if the vision might return as the Lady said. They
waited all morning in front of Lucia's house and asked her a hun-

dred questions about the original sighting. Becoming bitter from all the criticism, Lucia wondered if she should go at all. It was the Feast Day of St. Anthony, and Lucia usually loved the celebrations. Her mother asked her if she would waste this time to run up to the hills to see an imaginary Lady. Maria Carreira, a neighbor and friend, was one of the onlookers who joined the children, and she later became custodian of the shrine to Our Lady of Fatima.

At noon the apparition of the Lady appeared just as she promised. She was surrounded by a brilliant light and looked exactly like the first vision. But the village people who came to see her saw only a small white cloud float down from the Eastern sky and hover over the holm oak where the children were praying. The vision of the lady was not visible to anyone but the children.

Lucia asked in a trembling voice, "My Lady, what do you want of me?"

"I want you to come here on the thirteenth day of next month and pray the rosary every day, and I want you to learn to read."

Lucia asked for the cure of a sick woman and the Lady said if she was converted she would be cured within the year.

"I want you to take us to Heaven," Lucia asked simply.

"Yes," the Lady answered, "I will take Jacinta and Francisco soon, but you must remain on earth for some time. Jesus wishes to use you to make me better known and loved. He wishes to establish in the world devotion to my Immaculate Heart.

Lucia was saddened by the news. "Must I stay here alone?"

"No, my child. And would that make you suffer? Do not be disheartened. My Immaculate Heart will never abandon you, but will be your refuge and the way that will lead you to God."

The beautiful Lady opened her hands over the children and blessed them with immense rays of brilliant light that engulfed them. Francisco and Jacinta seemed to be covered in a beam of light that rose up toward heaven and Lucia was illuminated by a stream of light that radiated out over the world ending on the horizon.

In the palm of the Lady's right hand, the children saw a Heart surrounded by a wreath of thorns which pierced it many times. They understood this to be the Immaculate Heart of Mary, grieved by the sins of humanity and seeking reparation.

The Lady rose into the sky and drifted away. Maria claimed that she heard the sound of a rocket far away and saw a white cloud disappear as Francisco stood up and said, "There she goes."

The leaves of the holm oak were bent in the direction that the apparition went and remained so for several hours afterwards, as if someone had been standing on the branches. The villagers who accompanied the children saw only the bent leaves and the white cloud.

Lucia's mother was even more furious when she heard of the new sighting. The next morning she marched Lucia off to the priest in hopes that the priest could force her to tell the truth. The priest warned Lucia that the devil was at work here and she needed to be wary. He said that she should pray hard and give up going to the place of the visions or else her soul might be dammed forever.

Lucia's sisters and other family members had turned against her, too. At times the pain from her family's rejection was so great that she wanted to die. But she offered her pain up to Jesus for the reparation of the sins of others and to save souls and doing this gave her comfort. But she suffered terrible nightmares depicting the devil. Fearing damnation, she stopped praying the rosary, doing penance, and making sacrifices for the sins of others. She stayed away from Jacinta and Francisco. She even vowed to herself that she would never go to the Cova da Iria again.

As the 13th of July neared, Lucia hid herself away from others as much as possible but still suffered daily beatings from her mother. On the morning of the 13th many people gathered in the remote village of Fatima from all parts of the country to go to the Holy place. Only an hour before noon, Lucia felt a strong compulsion to go to the Cova da Iria after all. She ran by the house of Jacinta and Francisco and was surprised that they were still there. "We didn't dare go without you," said Jacinta, sobbing because of her worry.

They ran up into the hills accompanied by Ti Marto and Olympia, Jacinta and Francisco's parents. Over five thousand people had crowded around the hollow where the holm oak stood. When the children arrived, two huge men parted the pilgrims to make a path for them. The children immediately fell to their knees in front of the oak and said the rosary.

Minutes later Lucia cried out, "Shut your umbrellas. The Lady is coming." Everyone obeyed, but the hot sun was fierce and the unforgiving light bore down on their bare heads.

Everyone watched in silence as a white cloud drifted in and settled over the holm oak and the praying children. Instantly, the air cooled, and the sun dimmed, giving the people some relief from the intense July heat. This action amazed the pilgrims, who made notice of it later.

Lucia asked the apparition, "What do you want of me?"

"I want you to come here on the thirteenth day of next month and to continue to pray the rosary every day in honor of Our Lady of the Rosary, in order to obtain peace for the world and the end of the war (World War I), for she alone can help."

Lucia said meekly, "I would like to ask who you are and to perform a miracle so that people will believe that you are appearing to us."

"Continue to come here every month," the Lady replied.

"In October I will tell you who I am and what I want. And I will perform a miracle so that everyone may see and believe."

The Lady looked very grave and said, "Sacrifice yourselves for sinners and say often, especially when you make some sacrifice: `O my Jesus, this is for love of You, for the conversion of sinners, and in reparation for the offenses committed against the Immaculate Heart of Mary.'" At these words, she opened her hands on the three children once again. The light streaming from them seemed to penetrate the earth, opened it, and revealed to the children a vision of Hell. Lucia cried out in terror, calling upon Our Lady.

"We could see a vast sea of fire," Lucia confessed many years later. "Plunged in the flames were demons and lost souls, as if they were red-hot coals, transparent and black or bronze-colored, in human form, which floated about in the conflagration, borne by the flames which issued from them, with clouds of smoke falling on all sides as sparks fell in a great conflagration without weight or equilibrium, amid shrieks and groans of sorrow and despair that horrified us and caused us to tremble with fear. The devils could be distinguished by horrible and loathsome forms of animals, frightful and unknown, but transparent like black coals that have turned red-hot."

The children were full of fear at the sight. But the Lady spoke tenderly to them, "You saw Hell where the souls of poor sinners go. In order to save them, God wishes to establish in the world devotion to my Immaculate Heart. If people do what I ask, many souls will be saved and there will be peace. The war is going to end. But if people do not stop offending God, another, even worse, will begin in the reign of Pius XI. When you see a night illuminated by an unknown light, know that it is the great sign that God gives you that He is going to punish the world by means of war, hunger and persecution of the Church and of the

Holy Father. To prevent it, I shall come to ask for the consecration of Russia to my Immaculate Heart and the Communion of reparation on the first Saturdays.

If people attend to my requests, Russia will be converted and the world will have peace. If not, Russia will spread its errors throughout the world, fermenting wars and persecutions of the Church. The good will be martyred, the Holy Father will have much to suffer, and the various nations will be annihilated. In the end, my Immaculate Heart will triumph. The Holy Father will consecrate Russia to me; it will be converted and a certain period of peace will be granted to the world. In Portugal, the dogmas of the Faith will always be kept. . . " (here the third secret was revealed). The Lady asked that her words be kept secret.

Then she said, "When you say the rosary, say after each mystery: `O my Jesus, forgive us our sins, save us from the fires of Hell and lead all souls to Heaven, especially those most in need.'"

After a pause Lucia said, "Do you want anything more of me?"

"No," the Lady replied. "Today, I want nothing else of you."

Afterward Ti Marto remembered, "There was a sort of thunderclap and the little arch which had been put up over the holm oak to hang lanterns on shook as if in an earthquake. Lucia got up off her knees so quickly that her skirts ballooned out around her, and pointing towards the sky, she shouted, "There she goes." The villagers watched as the little white cloud hovering over the trees melted away.

Immediately, the crowd of onlookers engulfed the children, shouted questions at them about the vision and pushed close enough to touch their clothes. Ti Marto quickly grabbed Jacinto, and two other men carried Lucia and Francisco up the steep hill away from the crowds of people, and safely out of their reach.

But before she left, Lucia told the throngs of people that the Lady would return and give miraculous signs on the 13th of October, and that they should return then.

The administrator of the township was very angry after hearing the rumors about the apparition and sent word that the children should appear at a certain hour to be questioned by the court in the town of Vila Nova de Ourem, nine miles away from Fatima and a long way on foot. Lucia's parents felt she should appear and accept responsibility for her actions. Ti Marto called to say he would accompany Lucia and her father, but his children, Jacinto and Francisco, would not be going. The trip was too long for such young children.

Lucia was upset that her parents didn't protect her the way Ti Marto protected his children. She also feared that she might be harmed, but trusted that the Holy Lady would protect her.

The administrator, Author Santos, viciously questioned Lucia in front of her father and several other men about the miracles at Fatima and the "secrets" that had been revealed to her. Santos panicked and tried to force Lucia to confess by threatening her with many different penalties, including imprisonment and death. He was a weasel of a man. But the ten-year-old child never revealed the truth or gave in to her fears even though the man terrified her. She silently prayed that the Holy Lady would protect her. Filled with rage Santos turned to Ti Marto and repremanded him for not bringing Francisco and Jacinta to be interrogated. Santos paced angrily back and forth across the room warning them all that he had not given up, and they would hear from him again. He also forbade the children from ever going to the Cova da Iria again.

Many believed Author Santos to be a Communist, political activist, and atheist and suspected that word of the miracles at Fatima threatened his political aspirations. They knew he would stop at nothing to squelch "fictitious rumors and lies."

Lucia's daily beatings from her mother continued and even increased because all the pasture land and family vegetable gardens in the small fertile pocket of the Cova da Iria had been trampled by the pilgrims and the animals they brought with them. Most of the visitors arrived at the Cova da Iria either by foot, horse drawn wagon, or carriage.

"How are we to live without the food!" her mother shouted. But Lucia bore her no resentment and forgave her these furious outbursts.

August

On the 13th of August crowds of people poured into the little town of Fatima from all parts of Portugal. Many people sought out the children, asking them questions about the Lady and giving them petitions for healing. Lucia, Jacinta, and Francisco were besieged by desperate people who sought favors and miracles for their family members. In the middle of the throng of villagers, a messenger brought word that Arthur Santos was waiting for the children at the house of Ti Marto and that they must go there immediately.

From the moment the administrator laid eyes on the children, he questioned them again about the miracles and reminded them of his order that they weren't to go to the Cova da Iria again. After ordering the fathers to take their children to the parish priest, Santos left. A carriage waited for the children at the Priests' rectory, and Santos ordered the children to get in, saying that he had a change of heart and would take them to the Cova himself. On the way, however, Santos told the driver to change directions, driving his horses hard to the city of Ourem where he held the children captive in his own house. There he continued to persecute them and tried to force them to tell him the "secret" the Lady gave to the children.

"If they kill us we will go straight to heaven," Jacinta repeated again and again to comfort herself and Lucia and Francisco.

A crowd of over 15,000 people had gathered at the Cova da Iria waiting for the children to arrive. Word sifted through the throngs of people that the children had been kidnapped and arrested.

Anger and rage swept through the crowd like fire through dry brush and a riot would have broken out, but at that moment a huge clap thundered out over the hills.

"It seemed to be like the end of the world," said one eye witness. A blinding flash of light followed which stunned the crowd into silence. While looking up into the sky, the pilgrims witnessed a small white cloud drift gently down from the east and rest on top of the holm oak, where the children had seen the other apparitions.

A family friend, Maria de Carreira, described the event:

"I was not afraid. I knew there was nothing evil about the apparitions because if there were, the people would not be praying at the Cova. My constant prayer as I walked along was: `May Our Lady guide me according to God's Holy Will.' The crowd at the Cova on 13 August was even larger than in July. About eleven o'clock, Lucia's sister, Maria dos Anjos, came with some candles to light around the tree of Our Lady. The people prayed and sang religious hymns around the holm oak. The absence of the children made them very restless. When it became known that the magistrate had kidnapped them, a terrible resentment rippled through the crowd. There is no telling what it might have turned into, had it not thundered just then. Some thought the thunder came from the road; others thought it came from the holm oak;

but it seemed to me that it came from a distance. It frightened us all and many began to cry, fearing they were going to be killed, but no one was.

"Right after the thunder came a flash, and immediately, we all noticed a little cloud, very white, beautiful and bright, that came and stayed over the holm oak. It remained a few minutes, then rose toward the heavens where it disappeared. Looking about, we noticed a strange sight that we had already seen and would see again. Everyone's face glowed rose, red, blue —all the colors of the rainbow. The trees seemed to have no branches or leaves, but were all covered with flowers; every leaf was a flower. The ground was in little squares, each one a different color. Our clothes seemed to be transformed also into the colors of the rainbow. The two vigil lanterns hanging from the arch over the holy spot above the holm oak appeared to be turned into gold."

At that moment it was clear to the people that the Virgin Mary was able to manifest her miracles in front of thousands of people without the help of the children. Fearing retribution from the people, the Parish Priest denied that he assisted in the kidnapping of the children in any way. He went so far as to print a long letter in the next morning paper describing exactly what happened to the children and saying that he was blameless.

Obsessed with finding out the "secret" the Lady told the children, Santos didn't give up. When the children refused to talk, he had them thrown into prison like common criminals. Jacinta and Francisco sobbed the whole time through their constant prayers, unable to stop their tears. Santos wasn't moved to pity for the children's well being, but instead threatened time and time again to kill them if they didn't confess. Santos even threatened to throw them into boiling water, but that didn't change their minds. Jacinta said the rosary and her Hail Marys in front of him, provoking him to a terrible fury. Immediately, he had her dragged away. As she was taken out, Francisco prayed that her soul would go to heaven. When the guard returned a few minutes later, he told Santos in front of Lucia and Francisco that Jacinta was dead. Lucia and Francisco prayed all the harder, and then Francisco was dragged out. When the guard returned, he confessed that the little boy, Francisco, was dead also. Still Lucia didn't give in to the terrible threats and questioning. She thought only of going to heaven, if it was her time to go. She had forgotten that the Holy Lady said that she would live a long life. Lucia was so frightened and weak from not eating that when the guard touched her, she felt her body go limp and didn't recover until she saw the live faces of Jacinta and Francisco staring down at her when she was returned to the prison cell. Rejoicing that they were still alive, she hugged each one over and over. Finally, Santos gave up his inquisition and took the children back home to Fatima.

The children arrived home on the 15th of August, having missed the 13th all together. Lucia's parents were still angry at her for telling stories and didn't even give her a day of rest after the ordeal, but sent her immediately up to the hills with the sheep. On the other hand, the parents of Jacinta and Francisco wouldn't let them out of their sight and sent an older brother up into the hills to tend the sheep for several days. Even after all the miracles on the 13th, Lucia's mother said that if just one more person admitted to seeing the apparition and strange lights, then she might believe too.

The following Sunday on the 19th of August, Lucia took her sheep up into the hills to graze just as she did every day. But this day they were about a mile from Fatima in a place called Valinhos. Francisco and his brother John came with her, leaving Jacinta at home. Suddenly, the air grew strangely calm, an extraordinary atmospheric phenomena that had come before the visions in the Cova da Iria. A flash of light cut through the sky, and Lucia immediately sent John down the valley to get Jacinta. She knew the Lady would be coming there soon. When Jacinta arrived, another flash of light lit up the horizon, and the Lady appeared illuminated in a brilliant white light and stood on a nearby tree. John was disappointed that he didn't see anything.

The Lady urged the children to continue to go to the Cova on the thirteenth of the month and to pray the rosary every day. She repeated her promise to perform miracles on the 13th of October.

Then she repeated her request:

"Pray, pray a great deal and make many sacrifices, for many souls go to Hell because they have no one to make sacrifices and to pray for them." She complained about the ill treatment to which the children had been subjected and said that on account of this, the miracle intended for October would be less great. She then added that in October, "St. Joseph too will come with the Holy Child to bring peace to the world. Our Lord will also come to bless the people. Our Lady of the rosary and Our Lady of Sorrows will come too."

Shortly afterwards, the vision rose in a cloud of light and quickly disappeared. The children noticed that the branches of the tree on which she stood exuded a wonderful fragrance. They picked some branches as a testimony and hurried back home. Jacinta excitedly explained to Lucia's mother what had happened and then encouraged her to smell the branches they brought back. For the first time, Maria Rosa began to wonder if the children had been telling the truth after all.

September 13

Word had spread throughout Portugal about the miracles at Cova da Iria, and by the morning of September 13 hundreds of people crowded the streets, hills, and pastures around the Cova. This time there were many priests from the church to witness the sights.

Around noon the sun became dim until the stars were visible as on July 13. Then the Lady appeared in a white cloud and glided to the top of what remained of the holm oak. The children remained kneeling and prayed at the base of the tree just as they always did. Suddenly there was a rain of colorful rose petals, which vanished when they reached the ground. Then Lucia cried out, "Pray! You must pray!"

An eyewitness said: "Never will I forget the deep impression made on me by the sight of all these thousands of pilgrims falling on their knees at the voice of a child of ten and in tears praying and imploring with confidence the maternal protection of the Queen of Heaven."

The Lady told Lucia to continue to pray the rosary every day in order to hasten the end of the war. "In October our Lord will also come, and Our Lady of sorrows and of Mount Carmel and St. Joseph with the Child Jesus will come to bless the world."

Ever since the children saw the fiery pit of Hell, they had been wearing a rough rope tied around their waists to cause pain and pulled it so tight at times that they could barely breathe, offering this suffering up to the Holy Mother for the reparation of sins and for the saving of souls. But at this sighting, the Lady specifically asked them not to use the rope at night any more.

Lucia asked the Lady to cure some of the sick people whose petitions had been given to her. The Holy Mother said that some she would cure and others she wouldn't, but in October to expect to see many miracles.

Lucia's mother, Maria Rosa, still didn't believe the children's stories nor the story of the other onlookers and continued to beat Lucia with a broomstick for her lies and for the destruction of their property. Lucia again offered this abuse up to the Holy Mother for the reparation of sins and forgave her mother's ignorance. But in the midst of all this confusion of people asking to speak with Lucia, Maria Rosa was compelled to sell the flock of sheep because they no longer had a place to graze. This act posed a hardship on the poor family for the loss of food and wool.

October 13, 1917

Fifty thousand people from all over the world descended on Fatima and the Cova da Iria to witness the miracles predicted to occur on the thirteenth. The people represented all walks of life: rich, poor, priests, atheists, skeptics and believers, all hoping for a story they could tell their grandchildren.   Newspaper reporters wanted to disprove the tales of prophesy, miraculous occurrences and doom. Spectators were not disappointed. Driving rain flooded the roads and created a sea of mud that was practically impassible, but still the crowds of people came. Jacinta's father waded through two feet of water to carry her to the spot under what was left of the holm oak after souvenir seekers had taken its branches. Lucia and Francisco were also carried by men through the pressing crowd to the Holy Tree. In the driving rain Lucia asked the people to shut their umbrellas and look toward the sky.

Lucia cried out to the crowd, "Put down your umbrellas everyone!" Then to Jacinta and Francisco she whispered, "Kneel down. Our Lady is coming! I have seen the flash! A white mist developed around the children and rose to a height of almost fifteen feet.

Lucia asked, "What do you want of me?"

The Lady glowed in a brilliant light just as she had during

the other visitations, but the crowd saw only the heavenly signs created for their belief.

"I am the Lady of the Rosary," the apparition said. "I would like a chapel built here in my honor. Continue to pray the rosary every day. She added that the war would be ending soon and the soldiers would not be long returning to their homes."

Lucia asked favors for the numerous requests of healing that she had been given. The Lady said that she would grant some, but the most important was that men must amend their lives and ask pardon for their sins." Her last plea was, "Do not offend God anymore, for He is already too greatly offended."

As the Lady rose, beams of light radiated out from her hands reflecting on the sun. As she rose, the reflection of her own light continued to be projected on the sun itself.

Lucia shouted, "Look at the sun!" prompted by an inner impulse to do so.

After the Lady disappeared into the firmament, the children beheld St. Joseph carrying the Child Jesus in his arms, and Our Lady robed in white with a blue mantle covering her head, standing beside the sun. St. Joseph and the Child Jesus blessed the world as they traced the sign of the cross with their hands. Then in a few minutes this apparition disappeared and Lucia saw Our Lord and Our Lady, who seemed to be Our Lady of Dolours. Our Lord blessed the world in the same way that St. Joseph had done. This apparition also vanished, and they saw Our Lady once more. This time, though, the vision of the Lady resembled Our Lady of Carmel holding up a brown scapular to the world. The spirit of Carmel signifies triumph over suffering.

The people didn't see the apparitions that the children saw, but witnessed the miracle of the twentieth century. The following quotations were excerpted from the book *Fatima: The Great Sign*, by Francis Johnston.

"The black rain clouds separated, and exposed the full sun, which resembled a "mother of pearl" moon and could be looked at with the naked eye. In the next few minutes the sun moved back and forth across the sky and threw out great beams of colors in squares which checkered the earth and the people in different shades of the rainbow. The sun continued moving until it whirled like a gigantic fire wheel sending colored light beams in all directions. Then, just as suddenly as the movement began, it stopped. In no more than a few seconds the sun began again the movement of up and down, around in a circle, glowing more brilliantly than ever before and sending out over the countryside a spectrum of colors, first amethyst, then dark yellow, white and blue, according to eye witness reports. The crowd watched as if in a stupor for almost twelve minutes. Then without warning the sun plunged toward the earth and frightened the people so much they fell to the ground pleading for mercy and praying for forgiveness for their sins. In a terrifying moment the sun stopped just before it hit the earth and rose back up into its orbit. The pilgrims were so relieved to be alive that they all cried and prayed in thanksgiving. A few moments passed before they realized that their clothes were completely dry and free of the previous clinging mud. The earth and everything around them had been dried from the heat of the powerful sun.

When the sun's activity was over, the three children were besieged with questions and people pulling apart pieces of their clothing for souvenirs. To get the children away from the crowds, several big men hoisted them up over their heads, high above the pilgrims, as they carried them away.

When Lucia reached home, she realized that her long, waist-length braided hair not only had become lose, but was gone. In its place a short bob stared back at her from the mirror. Her hair was now shorter than Francisco's crop. Along the way people must have cut her long braids to keep as relics. At first Lucia was very upset, wondering how the people could cut her hair. But later, she admitted to herself that even her body belonged to God. If taking her hair helped the people believe, then she didn't mind.

Many miraculous healings were reported that day. One woman whose husband recovered from eczema fulfilled a promise she made to God before the cure by walking 300 yards on her knees to thank the Virgin of Fatima. Years later, in 1938 a man who was paralyzed on the left side came to Fatima to scoff at God's power to heal. Suddenly, he fainted. When he revived, he got up and immediately walked off, completely healed of his paralysis, and has remained healed ever since.

The Lady of Fatima's predictions that Francisco and Jacinta would die soon came true too. In December 1918 Francisco and Jacinta contracted Spanish influenza, which claimed the lives of 20 million people all over the world. Until the end Francisco prayed the rosary and offered his painful suffering up to the Lord for the reparation of the sins of others and to please God. Even in the last hours before his death, he was moved by the sad countenance that he had seen on the Lord's face. He asked that all his sins be forgiven and saw a beautiful light beside his door the day before he died on April 4, 1919.

Jacinta was failing fast, too, but she continued to pray the rosary and never tired of telling God that she loved Him. "My God, I love Thee in thanksgiving for all the graces Thou hast granted me. O my Jesus, I love Thee."

In December of 1919, Our Lady appeared again to Jacinta and asked if she would like to convert more sinners. Even in her weakened state, Jacinta happily said, "Yes," though she did not know what was ahead of her. The Lady told her that she would go to a hospital in Lisbon and suffer a great deal there. But again Jacinta was told that she should offer her suffering for the conversion of poor sinners and in reparation for offenses made against the Immaculate Heart of Mary and that she would die all without family or friends in Lisbon. The Lady also said that Jacinta wouldn't be completely alone, but that the Blessed Virgin would always be by her side.

Several days after the vision when the priests discovered Jacinta still terribly ill from the influenza, they decided to send her to the hospital in Lisbon so that she would receive the finest medical care available. Her family was too poor to send anyone to stay with her, so Jacinta, who was ten-years-old, was sent alone, just as The Lady had prophesied.

Once in Lisbon, Jacinta lived in an orphanage and was attended by Sister Mother Godinho. The Lady of Fatima appeared to her there several times more. The following quotes are also from the book *Fatima: The Great Sign.* The information was given to the church by Sister Mother Godinho who remained at Jacinto's side until she died.

"At one appearance the Lady told Jacinta, 'The sins of the world are very great. If men only knew what eternity is, they would do everything in their power to change their lives. You must pray much for sinners, priests and the religious; priests must concern themselves with only the things of the church. Fly from riches and luxury. Love poverty and silence. Have charity even for bad people. Confession is a sacrament of mercy, and we must confess with joy and trust. Disobedience of our priests and religious gravely displeases our Lord. Many marriages are not of God and do not please the Lord. Many fashions will be introduced which will give great offense to God. Let men avoid greed, lies, envy, blasphemy, impurity. The mother of God wants more virgin souls bound by the vow of chastity. Woe to women wanting in modesty. Never speak ill of anyone. Never complain or murmur. Be very patient, for patience leads to heaven.'"

Jacinta also revealed that the Lady said, "Wars are punishment for sin. Our Lady can no longer uphold the arm of our Divine Son which will strike the world. If people amend their lives, Our Lord will even now save the world, but if they do not, punishment will come."

Jacinta's condition continued to decline, and she was admitted to the Hospital at Lisbon on February 2, 1920, for purulent pleurisy. Eight days later she was operated on, and the doctors removed two infected ribs with only the use of local anesthetic. She never complained of the excruciating pain, but she was heard saying, "Now you can convert many sinners for I suffer much."

After suffering terrible pain, Jacinta died on February 20, 1920. All that day the nurses heard the child pleading with God to accept her pain as penance for hardened sinners. When the nurse found her dead, there were tears of blood on her little cheeks. She died alone just as the Lady had said. Thousands of mourners visited Lisbon and the Church of Angels to pay their last respects to Jacinta. They were not disappointed because many noticed an unusual fragrance never witnessed before when they passed by her coffin. Some said it was a scent from heaven. Even the confirmed skeptics were stunned by the unmistakable sweet aroma. To this day many pilgrims to her grave have witnessed the same sweet heavenly scent.

On September 12, 1935, the mortal remains of Jacinta were exhumed, and much to the surprise of the priests, they were still intact. Even her facial features were visible and her skin softly drawn over her bones. When the remains of the child Francisco were exhumed, the priests found only bones. His body was exposed to the same lye bath that Jacinta's body received as this was the usual burial custom in Portugal in the early 1900s. Jacinta's body has been miraculously preserved as have the bodies of other Saints.

Lucia missed her cousins desperately. She did receive word,

however, that before Jacinta died, the Lady told her the exact day and hour of her death. Two of the secret prophecies the Lady of Fatima predicted had come true. These were the deaths of Jacinta and Francisco and the end of World War I. Lucia wondered what would befall the world now if the people didn't repent. Would a terrible war follow? Would there be a second world war? The third secret was not revealed, but Lucia gave the information in a letter to the Pope, who kept the secret safe and said the Vatican would reveal it in 1960. In 1960 the Pope read the secret to the Cardinals and decided not to reveal its message to the public at that time.

Because Lucia was continually besieged by pilgrims questioning her about the miracles and the prophecies that she witnessed, the priests decided to change her name and send her away to a convent school. With her parent's permission, Lucia was sent to a school near Oporto. In 1925, she entered the Order of St. Dorothy at Tuy, just over the Spanish border.

Lucia continued to have visions during her life. The following excerpts are from the book, *Fatima: In Lucia's Own Words, Sister Lucia's Memoirs*. The following is the written confession Lucia made to her priest in 1931 about a vision she received from Jesus and the Virgin concerning the Consecration of Russia in 1925. This was written by the priest.

"On December 10, 1925, the most Holy Virgin appeared to her and, by her side, elevated on a luminous cloud, was a Child. The most Holy Virgin rested her hand on Lucia's shoulder, and when she did so, she showed Lucia with the other hand her immaculate heart encircled with thorns.

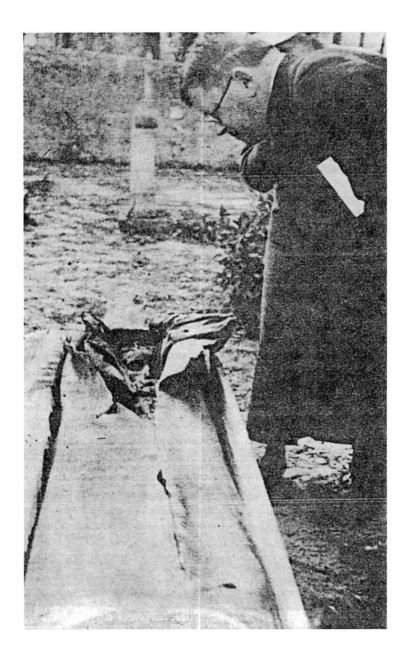

THE MORTAL REMAINS OF JACINTA

"At the same time the Holy Child said, 'Have compassion on the Heart of your most Holy Mother covered with thorns, with which ungrateful men pierce it every day, and there is no one to make an act of reparation to remove them.'"

"Then the most Holy Virgin said, 'Look, my daughter, at my Heart, surrounded in thorns with which ungrateful men pierce me at every moment by their blasphemies and ingratitude. You at least try to console me and say that I promise to assist at the hour of death, with the graces necessary for salvation, all those who, on the first Saturday of five consecutive months, shall confess, receive Holy Communion, recite five decades of the Rosary, and keep me company for fifteen minutes while meditating on the fifteen mysteries of the Rosary, with the intention of making reparation to me.'"

"On the 15th of February 1926, the Infant Jesus appeared to Lucia again. He asked if she had already spread the devotion to His most Holy Mother? Lucia told Him of the confessor's difficulties and said that Mother Superior was prepared to propagate it, but that the confessor had said that she, alone, could do nothing.

"Jesus replied: 'It is true that your Superior alone can do nothing, but with my grace she can do all.'"

"Lucia told Jesus that some people don't want to confess on Saturday, and asked if it might be valid to go to confession within eight days.

"Jesus answered, 'Yes, and it could be longer still, provided that, when they receive me, they are in the state of grace and have the intention of making reparation to the Immaculate Heart of Mary.'"

"She then asked, 'My Jesus, what about those who forget to make this intention?'"

"Jesus replied, 'They can do so at their confession, taking

advantage of the first opportunity to go.'"

Rev. Fr. José Bernardo Goncalves, S. J., the seers spiritual director, copied this document from Lucia's own handwriting.

Request for the Consecration of Russia

"On June 13, 1929, the Holy Lady of Fatima came to Lucia and informed her that it was time to make the second secret—the request for the Consecration of Russia—public.

Lucia's confession follows:

"'I had sought and obtained permission to make a Holy Hour from eleven o'clock until midnight every Thursday and Friday night. Being alone one night, I knelt near the altar rails in the middle of the chapel and, prostrate, I prayed the prayers of the Angel. Feeling tired, I then stood up and continued to say the prayers with my arms in the form of a cross. The only light was

"On June 13, 1929, the Holy Lady of Fatima came to Lucia and informed her that it was time to make the second secret—the request for the Consecration of Russia—public.

Lucia's confession follows:

"'I had sought and obtained permission to make a Holy Hour from eleven o'clock until midnight every Thursday and Friday night. Being alone one night, I knelt near the altar rails in the middle of the chapel and, prostrate, I prayed the prayers of the Angel. Feeling tired, I then stood up and continued to say the prayers with my arms in the form of a cross. The only light was that of the sanctuary lamp. Suddenly the whole chapel was illumined by a supernatural light, and above the altar appeared a cross of light reaching to the ceiling. In a brighter light on the upper part of the cross could be seen the face of a man and His body as far as the waist. On His breast was a dove of light; nailed to the cross was the body of another man. A little below the waist,

I could see a chalice and a large Host suspended in the air, onto which drops of blood were falling from the face of Jesus Crucified and from the wound on His side. These drops ran down onto the host and fell into the chalice. Beneath the right arm of the cross was Our Lady, and in Her hand was Her Immaculate Heart. (It was Our Lady of Fatima, with Her Immaculate Heart in her left hand, without sword or roses, but with a crown of thorns and flames). Under the left arm of the cross, large letters, as if of crystal clear water which ran down upon the altar, formed these words: `Grace and Mercy.'

"I understood that the Mystery of the Most Holy Trinity was shown to me, and I received enlightenments about this mystery which I am not allowed to reveal.

"Our Lady then said to me:

"`The moment has come in which God asks the Holy Father, in union with all the Bishops of the world, to make the Consecration of Russia to my Immaculate Heart, promising to save it by this means. There are so many souls whom the justice of God condemns for sins committed against me, that I have come to ask reparation: sacrifice yourself for this intention and pray.'"

This request from the Lady of Fatima came as a direct response to the second secret given to the children on July 13, 1917. The Consecration of Russia was to precede a cataclysmic tragedy of the second world war. Even though the Holy Father at the time knew of the secrets of Fatima, he was unable to convince the Bishops to comply with this direct order from the Lady. Perhaps they didn't believe in Lucia's visions and prophecies. At the time Russia was in turmoil and involved with a civil war between the Reds and the Whites and not available to provide council on the matter. But when the Czar Nicholas abdicated in March 1917, the fate of Russia was left to the Communists. No longer was a religious sovereign in charge. Whatever the reason, the

Holy Lady's request for the Bishops to Consecrate Russia to the Immaculate Heart was not carried out. Jesus came to Lucia several years later in a vision saying:

"In an intimate communication, our Lord complained to me saying:"

"'They did not wish to heed my request. Like the King of France, they will repent and do it, but it will be late. Russia will have already spread her errors throughout the world, provoking wars, and persecutions of the Church: the Holy Father will have much to suffer.'" *Fatima: Lucia's Own Words*.

Just as predicted, a great light appeared over Europe and the Northern Hemisphere on January 25-26, 1938, from 9 pm to 2 am. It was so spectacular that the *New York Times* attributed it to an exceptional aurora borealis and devoted an entire page to it. But this light was the same light the Lady of Fatima predicted would be a sign beginning a great war, God's punishment to man. The Lady also said the war would begin during the pontification of Pius XI. As early as 1936 Hitler invaded the Rhineland. Pope Pius XI reigned from 1922-39. In March 1938 Hitler declared war on Austria, beginning World War II, the world's most horrible and devastating War and annihilation of people. Was this war the direct result of a world who refused to pray and turn their lives over to God? We can only speculate.

The Lady of Fatima predicted that after Russia was Consecrated to the Immaculate Heart of Mary, there would be a period of peace in the world. In 1942 Pope Pius XII prayed that all Christians pray and Consecrate the whole world to the Immaculate Heart of Mary, not just Russia. A few days later came the turning point of World War II according to Sir Winston Churchill.

Over the years there have been many Popes who have interpreted the directions from the Lady of Fatima. But the most important message from Fatima is for each person to pray for the peace of the world and offer up their suffering for the reparation of the sins of others. Then and only then will eternal peace prevail.

In 1989 the first election to occur in Russia since March 1917, took place and Mikhail S. Gorbachev was elected the first president. Russia became a democracy where religious practices were finally accepted nationwide. Almost overnight a great communist nation and people of many beliefs converted to the Christian faith, again fulfilling a Fatima prophecy.

The third secret of Fatima has never been revealed. Instructions were given the Pope to read and make public the contents of Lucia's letter in 1960. Pope John XXIII did read the message to his Cardinals, but the ecclesiastical authorities decided not to make the contents known to the general public.

In 1998 Sister Lucia celebrated her 90th birthday and was still living in a convent in Portugal. To this day the Third secret has not been made public. Perhaps since Russia has been Consecrated to the Immaculate Heart of Mary, we will see peace for some years as predicted. But Sister Lucia has spent her life sending petitions to Popes, Bishops, Cardinals and others begging for them to follow the requests of the Lady of Fatima.

Bibliography

Kondor, Louis, Fr., editor. *Fatima In Lucia's Own Words, Sister Lucia's Memoirs.* Postulation Centre, Fatima, Portugal, 1924.

Johnston, Francis. *Fatima: The Great Sign.* Tan Books and Publishers, Inc., Rockford, Illinois, 1980, p. 83,84,85.

Our Loving Mother's Children. *To Bear Witness that I AM the LIVING SON of GOD.* Our Loving Mother's Children, Newington, Virginia, 1991.

Life Magazine. "The Miracle of Fatima," December 20, 1948. p. 33-36.

MAP OF MEDJUGORJE

MFH Graphics

The Miracles at Medjugorje

Medjugorje is a tiny village in the province of Bosnia Hercegovina, Yugoslavia. On a country hillside in June 1981, the Blessed Virgin appeared in a vision to six children and pleaded for peace and reconciliation and in the world. She continued to appear to these six teenagers daily until 1985, when she reduced her appearances. Along with the Blessed Virgin's visits many miracles occurred, great miracles like the sun spinning in the sky, Jesus appearing, rosary chains turning to gold, beams of light flashing through the sky, and healing of the sick. The Virgin Mary's message has always been the same: "Pray for peace in the world and love each other." Some people think that Medjugorje is one of the most Holy spots on earth.

The village of Medjugorje lies at the base of Mount Krizavek, which means "Mountain of the Cross." Ever since 1933 the giant 36-foot-tall, concrete cross standing on top of Mt. Krizavek has towered over the many little villages at the mountain's base and has been an inspiration to the primarily Catholic community. Some feel the cross represents Jesus watching over them.

The demonstration of devotion to God by the villagers began years ago with the cross. The people of Medjugorje (Medjew-gor-yay), young and old, rich and poor, carried concrete and water a mile up the steep slopes of the mountain to build the concrete cross as a celebration and memorial honoring 1900 years since Jesus was crucified. Ever since the cross was erected, hundreds climb the steep mountain every year to pray and ask for miracles from Jesus. Many believe that the location is holy and often bring their sick to the base of the cross for healing. No one is sure how many actual healings have occurred there, but many troubled people have been inspired to meaningful religious conversion.

On the lovely summer afternoon of June 24, 1981, two young girls—Mirjana and Ivanka—went for a walk in the hills near their village, Bijakovici. Along the way they could see the St. James Church with Mount Krizevac behind it and the concrete cross towering over them. They were high enough up in the foothills of the mountain to look down on the other villages that checkered the landscape below and made up the parish of Medjugorje.

Ivanka, fourteen, spotted something shining on the hillside. Upon a second look, she thought she saw the form of "Our Lady." Mirjana, then sixteen, ignored Ivanka's story and refused to believe even a word of it. They returned to their village in silence. But later that day, around 6:00 pm, when the girls ventured back into the hills to gather their sheep, Mirjana clearly saw the vision, and Ivanka saw "Our Lady" for the second time.

"It really was Our Lady," Ivanka said later. "She held the baby Jesus on her arm. I saw a crown on her head, and she was wearing a long robe."

The girls ran back to the village to tell their friends Vicka and Ivan to join them. The next day, June 25, 1981, two more friends Maria and Jakov, were added to the group that went back to that same spot to see the Lady. They were not disappointed. The Virgin Mary appeared again in a beautiful light-filled cloud, and as she appeared, the young people were engulfed by an overwhelming sense of love and mercy. Ivanka asked about her mother, who had passed away two months earlier.

"She is happy. She is with me," Our Lady said.

The visionaries asked if Our Lady would return the next day. She responded with a nod. Later she said, "Good-bye, my angels. Go in the peace of God."

On June 26 nearly three thousand people were drawn to the hill by the luminary signs coming from that spot. When the vision appeared, the young girl, Vicka, sprinkled a bottle of Holy Water on Our Lady. She asked if the Lady was the Virgin Mary.

Our Lady only smiled.

"Why are you here? What do you want?" asked Ivanka.

"I have come because there are many true believers here. I wish to be with you to convert and to reconcile the whole world."

Every evening the Lady appeared, and eventually as word about the visions traveled throughout the country, crowds of people came from every direction. The Virgin Mother appeared on the hillside until the police intervened and tried to break up the crowd and stop the evening group. The communist laws strictly prohibited large gatherings in public and religious meetings were barely tolerated in the churches. The Mayor became worried about the influence the vision of the Virgin Mary had over the people and forbade the children from congregating on the hillside. The children were the only ones to see the Virgin, and they were being sought by the police. The communists refused to believe the sightings were real.

The Lady's message was simple: "I am the Queen of Peace. I have come to reconcile all people."

The parish priest, Father Jozo Zovko, OFM, organized prayers and an evening Mass in his church specifically for Our Lady. He prayed often and long for some insight into the origin of the vision. Late one afternoon, he received a direction from an inner voice: "Come out and protect the children."

He didn't know why he was directed to do so, but he obeyed and went outside. He was surprised to see the six young people running towards him.

"Hide us!" they cried. "The police are chasing us!"

He took them into the rectory just before the police arrived asking questions about the children. The police left, satisfied by his answers, and continued on their way to Bijakovici, not realizing that the children had hidden in the chapel. Because of his answered prayer, the Father knew that the visions were authentic.

Later on in the summer when the children had moved their prayers into the chapel, the Lady appeared to him and to the children. She did not speak to him, but he was a changed man. He knew the implications of the vision and how angry the Communist officials were about the religious sightings. From that moment on he knew his life was in danger. He told a priest who had been sent to help him, "Be prepared to take my place."

Not long after that vision, there was a police raid on the parish. Father Jozo was arrested, tried for sedition, and sentenced to three-and-a-half years in prison. By that time he had arranged for the children to meet in the sacristy, a small room off the main sanctuary. The Lady appeared to the children there every evening until 1985, when Bishop Pavao Zanie forbade it, afraid of the communists and wanting to appease their orders to squelch the visions. After that order the children moved their evening prayers to the parish house, where Our Lady has been appearing ever since.

Over the past seventeen years many apocalyptic signs have been seen by visitors to Medjugorje. Some have seen the sun spinning, visions of Mary and Christ, fire balls in the sky, unexplained lights, a frequent reference to the works of Satan, and predictions of great catastrophes and war. Others have witnessed the chains of their rosaries turn to gold and silver. Many healing miracles have occurred as well. Even with the dangers from the civil war between the Croats and the Serbs, pilgrims from all over the world travel to Medjugorje to receive a blessing from the Virgin and from Jesus and to pay their respects to God.

These young visionaries were chosen by the Virgin Mary and God to play a great part in the salvation of the world. They are not rich or well educated or even very sophisticated. They all have one thing in common; they have pure hearts and love the Virgin and Jesus Christ. Neither are they all perfect. They too have flaws, human flaws. But these were the ones who were chosen to receive the visions and with the Holy Spirit's help have been strong enough to withstand the abuse, disbelief, and criticism of thousands and stand fast for the Lord. They have been even stronger than the well-educated and pious priests and Bishops who have bent to the pressures from the atheistic communist politicians.

These visionaries have even more to bear. The Holy Mother has given them the burden to carry the secrets of the fate of the world and everyone in it.—the secrets about Armageddon. When the time is appointed, these young people are given the responsibility to tell the world when judgement day arrives. They will have God's protection and help, but each one must carry this burden alone. Already they know the dates when certain predictions will occur. These young visionaries are described in the following short biographies:

Ivanka Ivankovic-Elez was born on April 21, 1966. Even though she belongs to the province of Bijakovici, she lives at Mostar with her father, grandmother, brother, and sister. She has been keeping house for her family ever since her mother died in 1981. The Virgin Mary appeared to her first on the hillside on June 24, 1981. Her wedding was celebrated on December 28, 1986. As a devout Catholic she also prays every day for several hours. Our Lady told her that she will have an apparition on every June 25, the anniversary of the first vision. On May 7, 1985, Our Lady confided to her the last of ten secrets. Every year since, she has received a vision on June 25.

Marjana Dragicevic-Soldo was born on March 18, 1965. Her family lived in Sarajevo, where Mirjana studied agronomy. She was one of the first to see the Virgin on June 24, 1981. Her daily apparitions stopped on December 25, 1982. Our Lady gave Mirjana ten secrets and asked that they be kept sacred until the time appointed for them to be revealed to the world. After receiving the tenth secret and the final apparition, Our Lady told Mirjana that she would return to her every year on March 18, Mirjana's birthday. Mirjana was given a special blessing of receiving ten secrets from Our Lady and making the secrets known at the appointed time. During 1985 and 1986, she saw Our Lady and heard her voice a number of times when she was given the information about the secrets. Mirjana has been given the responsibility of choosing a priest to whom she will reveal the secrets. Mirjana will give the Priest a document on which the secrets are written, a document that the Holy Virgin will give to Mirjana. No one else can read the secret. The Priest will have seven days to pray and three more days to announce to the world what is to happen.

Marjana cries when she thinks of the first admonition to the world, which she has seen in a vision. The first time she heard the secret, she asked the Holy Mother, "Does it have to be like that?"

Our Lady's answer was, "Look at the way the world is living." (page 6) Medjugorje Journal.

Vicka Ivankovic was born on July 3, 1964. She has five sisters and two brothers and lives in Bijakovici. She suffers from severe headaches because of a non-malignant tumor. Our Lady appeared to her on June 24, 1981. Through her daily visions of the Virgin, she has received nine secrets. Prayer and fasting are integral parts of her life, and she is seriously considering being a nun. Praying and saying the rosary at least three or four hours a day are not unusual for Vika.

Maria Pavlovic-Lunetti was born April 1, 1965. She is also from a large family of three brothers and two sisters. Maria lives at home and helps when she can with pasturing the sheep. She tries to stay away from all the visitors seeking the visionaries. In 1998 she still received daily apparitions from Our Lady. On the 25th day of the month, she also received a message to give to the parish priest, the villagers, and the world. She has received nine of the secrets from Our Lady.

Ivan Dragicevic was born May 25, 1965. He is the eldest of three brothers. He farmed his father's land and attended, for a short time, the junior seminary, but the work was too difficult and he was forced to resign. In June of 1986 Ivan was drafted into the military. Our Lady appears to him also every day. She has confided nine secrets to him too. He is a very quiet person who still wants to become a priest and devoutly prays in the early morning and then in the evening for Mass and several hours later. The daily apparitions will stop when he receives the tenth secret.

Jakov Colo was born June 3, 1971, and lives with his uncle and aunt and their small girls. Both of his parents are dead. He is a student at a secondary school at Citluk. Our Lady has confided nine secrets to him, and he receives daily apparitions. His life has become one filled with devotion to God and he prays for several hours in the morning and again at Mass in the evening. He strives to live the life that the Virgin has set before him. One of love and mercy to his fellow man.

Two other girls are able to see the visions of the Virgin Mary. Jelena Vasilj who was born on May 14, 1972, and Marijana Vasilj, who is no relation, was born October 5, 1971.

When all the visionaries receive all ten secrets, the visitations from the Virgin Mary will cease, except for those whom she promised to visit once a year.

The Blessed Virgin appeared everyday to most of the visionaries until 1985, when she limited her appearances to only those who had not yet received all the secrets. Her messages and miracles number in the thousands and are on public record; many have been published in the books written about Medjugorje. The following communications from Our Lady were given to the teenagers during their evening prayers. Only a few of the highlights of the year 1981 are included.

June 26, 1981: While Mirjana was walking down the mountain, she was mysteriously pushed aside on the path by an unseen force. The virgin appeared to her again, this time carrying a wooden cross and crying, "Peace, Peace, Peace! Be reconciled! Only Peace. Make your peace with God among yourselves. For that it is necessary to believe, to pray, to fast, and to go to confession."

June 27, 1981: Mirjana and Jakov were upset because people were treating them like liars. Our Lady's response was, "My angels, do not be afraid of injustices. They have always existed."

"How must we pray?" the visionaries asked.

"Continue to recite the Lord's prayer, the Hail Mary, and the Glory Be seven times, but also add the Creed. Good-bye, my angels. Go in peace of God."

December 7, 1981: After Our Lady looked at the crowds,

Pray and persist in prayers."

When Jakov returned home the letters "Mir Ljudima" (Peace to the people) were on the wall in gold.

December 8, 1981: Our lady answered questions the visionaries had about their futures. "I would like all of you to become priests and religious, but only if you desire it. You are free. It is up to you to choose. If you are experiencing difficulties or if you need something, come to me. If you do not have the strength to fast on bread and water, you can give up a number of things. It would be a good thing to give up television, because after seeing some programs you are distracted and unable to pray. You can give up alcohol, cigarettes, and other pleasures. You yourselves know what you have to do."

July 22, 1981: The visionaries saw Jesus' head, brown eyes, beard, and long hair to prepare them for the suffering and persecution they were having to endure. "My angels, I send you my Son, Jesus, Who was tortured for His faith, and yet He endured everything. You also, my angels, will endure everything."

The visionaries were praised for their beautiful singing and praying. "It is beautiful to listen to you. Continue in this manner. Don't be afraid for Jozo."

October 1, 1981: Are all religions the same? "Members of all faiths are equal before God. God rules over each faith just like a sovereign over his kingdom. In the world, all religions are not the same because all people have not complied with the commandments of God. They reject and disparage them."

Are all churches the same? "In some, the strength of prayer to God is greater, in others, smaller. That depends on the priests who motivate others to pray. It depends also on the power which they have."

October 21, 1981: Vicka is worried about Fr. Jozo's sentencing and begs Her to intercede so that the people involved be reasonable and impartial.

"Jozo looks well and he greets you warmly. Do not fear for Jozo. He is a saint. I have already told you. Sentence will not be pronounced this evening. Do not be afraid. He will not be condemned to a severe punishment. Pray only, because Jozo asks from you prayer and perseverance. Do not be afraid because I am with you."

October 22, 1981: The visionaries asked if the whiteness of the cross is a supernatural phenomenon. "Yes, I confirm it."

Many saw the cross transform itself into a light and then into a silhouette of Our Lady. "All of these signs are designed to strengthen your faith until I leave you the visible and permanent sign."

October 25, 1981: The visionaries asked Our Lady about the great light three girls saw on their way home from Mass. Within the light, they saw fifteen figures. "It was a supernatural phenomenon. I was among the saints."

November 6, 1981: During this apparition, Our Lady disappeared and the visionaries saw a terrifying vision of Hell. Then Our Lady reappeared and said: "Do not be afraid! I have shown you Hell so that you may know the state of those who are there."

November 22, 1981: The Gospa (Our Lady in Yugoslavia) explains the cross, the heart, and the sun to the visionaries. "These are the signs of salvation: The cross is a sign of mercy, just like the heart. The sun is the source of light, which enlightens us."

Again a shining silhouette took the place of the cross on Krizevac. The visionaries asked the Blessed Virgin if it was She. "Why do you ask me, my angels? Have you not seen me? The world must find salvation while there is time. Let it pray with fervor. May it have the spirit of faith."

November 26, 1981: The visionaries asked the Gospa questions about the sick: "Have strong faith, pray, and fast and they will be cured. Be confident and rest in joy. Go in the peace of God. Be patient and pray for the cure. Good-bye, my dear angels."

December 31, 1981: Ivan asked the Gospa how to help doubting priests understand the apparitions. "It is necessary to tell them that from the very beginning I have been conveying the message of God to the world. It is a great pity not to believe in it. Faith is a vital element, but one cannot compel a person to believe. Faith is the foundation from which everything flows."

Ivan asked Our Lady if it was really She appearing at the foot of the cross. "Yes, it is true. Almost everyday, I am at the foot of the cross. My son carried the cross. He has suffered on the cross, and by it he saved the world. Everyday I pray to my Son to forgive the sins of the world."

Ten secrets have been given to all but two of the children, but none have been revealed to the public. The Holy Mother will tell them when it is time to reveal the secrets.

Message given to Mirjana from the Virgin Mother at Sarajevo, January 28, 1987. From the <u>Medjugorje Journal</u>, p. 199,200.

"Dear children, I have come to you to lead you to purity of soul, and so to God.

How have you listened to me? At the beginning without believing in fear and with distrust towards the girls and boys I have chosen. Then most of you welcomed me in your hearts and began to put into practice my motherly requests. However, this has not lasted very long.

Wherever I come, and with me my Son, Satan arrives too. Without being aware of it, you have allowed him to take the upper hand in you; he dominates you. At times you have understood that some of the things you do are not from God, but you quickly quell this feeling.

Don't allow this, my children! Dry the tears on my face which pour down, seeing your behavior. Look around you!

Take time to come to your God in church. Come to your Father's house.

Take time to get together in your family to implore grace from God.

Remember your dead. Give them joy with the celebration of the Mass.

Don't look with disdain at the poor who ask you for a crust of bread. Don't send them away from your plentiful table. Help them! And then God will help you. Perhaps the blessing, which he gives you in place of thanks will come about, perhaps God will hear it.

You, my children, have forgotten these things.

And Satan has influenced you also in this.

Don't let him. Pray with me! Don't deceive yourselves, thinking: "I am good, but my brother and sister beside me are worth nothing." This is not right.

I, as your Mother, love you; and therefore I admonish you.

There are secrets, my sons and daughters, which will remain unknown; but by the time you know it will be too late.

Return to prayer. Nothing is more important. I want the Lord to allow me to make clear even a little these secrets; but already the graces he offers you are too much.

Reflect on how much you offer him. When did you last give something up for the Lord?

I don't want to reproach you further; I want instead to invite you once again to prayer, to fasting, to penance.

If with fasting you desire to obtain grace from God, no one should know that you are fasting.

If with a gift to a poor person you want to receive grace from God, nobody should know of it, except you and the Lord.

from God, nobody should know of it, except you and the Lord.

Listen to me, my children; reflect in prayer on my message."

During the 1981 census in Yugoslavia, 22 million people were registered, eight million Serbs, four million Croats, four million Muslims and over one million each Slovenes and Macedonians, with half a million Montenegrans. In Yugoslavia the majority of the people—eight million—are of the Greek Orthodox religion, six million Catholics and four million Muslim.

In 1991, ten years after the first apparitions of the Virgin Mary, a bitter and destructive civil war began when the Serbs invaded Croatia and Bosnia Hercegovina. By 1996 many small villages lay in ashes.

In 1997 a business man was traveling through the town of Medjugorje in hopes of seeing the most "Holy" spot for Christians in the world. He was mortified that the villages had been reduced to ashes and his attention was drawn away from the cross on top of the mountain to two servicemen who had just been injured from a land mine explosion. His response was, "What a terrible act of blasphemy to a Holy landmark, its people, and ultimately to God." Millions of people suffered tortuous deaths, and those left behind are scarred forever by their terrible memories. But even after all this destruction, these young visionaries are still receiving messages from the Blessed Mother concerning the fate of the world.

Bibliography

Rooney, Lucy, SND; Faricy, Robert, SJ. *Medjugorje Journal.* Chicago, Illinois: Franciscan Herald Press, 1988. p. 129-200,

Weible, Wayne. *Medjugorje The Mission.* Orleans, Massachusetts: Paraclete Press, 1994.

Weible, Wayne. *Medjugorje The Message.* Orleans, Massachusetts: Paraclete Press, 19 1989.

LOCATION OF CONYERS IN GEORGIA

MFH Graphics

STATUE OF JESUS CRUCIFIED ON THE HOLY HILL AT CONYERS

Miracles at Conyers
cↄ⊙⊙ↄ

Are the Son of God, Jesus Christ, and his mother, the Virgin Mary, visiting with the humble housewife and mother Nancy Fowler? A woman who lived in a suburb of Atlanta, Georgia, claimed that Jesus and the Virgin Mary came to her daily and gave her messages for the salvation of the world. This news was hard for anyone to believe or ignore. True or not, this story carried enough weight for the news stations to broadcast it all over the state and eventually the country. The visions began in 1987 in Nancy's home when Jesus appeared before her and told her, "To bear witness I am the living Son of God."

A flurry of attention surrounded Nancy Fowler from the beginning. Some people believed her and became her devoted followers, attending the public visions on the thirteenth day of each month. Others complained that she just wanted to make money, and the visions were a hoax. Many said how sad it was to publicize the fact that the woman was quite crazy. In spite of all the doubting Thomases, word of her talks with Jesus and other miracles spread like a whirlwind from person to person. Soon Nancy was forced to move to Conyers, Georgia, an area large enough to accomodate the huge crowds. Within two years thousands from all over the country were visiting the religious site in Conyers, Georgia, on the 13th of each month to see Nancy and to hear her messages from the living Jesus.

Television stations broadcasted interviews from people who arrived before midnight on the 12th in order to get good seats for the next morning's teaching. Some days more than fifty thousand people crowded onto the few acres of sanctuary to pray at the Holy sites. Camera crews tried to document the appearances of Jesus in the clouds, but were disappointed. Newspaper articles reported that the number of pilgrims who had visited Conyers had reached a million. But few media personnel claimed that they had experienced any sightings or miracles themselves.

Almost ten years later in 1998 when I (the author) was receiving chemotherapy for cancer treatment, I heard the husband of a patient claim that his mother thought the sightings were real. She had witnessed rosary chains turn to gold and swore that other people saw the Virgin Mary appear in the clouds. Others witnessed a cross in the sky, illuminated by the sun, and smelled the aroma from fresh roses, a common sign of the presence of the Virgin Mary. After hearing these accounts, something in me wanted to believe these stories were true, so I decided to visit the site, hoping to find a miracle, too.

In order to avoid the crowds of people on the 13th, I went on the 12th of February. I easily found the two small brick ranch houses where Nancy Fowler lives and knocked on the door of the first one. There were large painted signs directing visitors to the Holy sights, but I wanted to talk to someone about Nancy and her visions while the place was all but deserted.

Carol Bradford, a volunteer, opened the door and excitedly told me of her encounters. She said the first time she prayed to the "Holy Mother" she felt a beam of warmth go right through her body, from her head to her toes. Immediately, a cloud of love surrounded her, and with it came a wonderful feeling of peace and forgiveness. Then she saw the face of Christ appear in the sky. He looked down on her with such powerful, loving eyes that she began to cry. That moment was the most extraordinary of her life. On other occasions she saw crosses in the sky and again felt covered with light-rays of love which radiated from the "Holy Mother Mary" statue. She has been volunteering in Conyers ever since, helping answer the phone and talking to visitors. She asked me to wait outside on the sidewalk, gave me a chair and said the Frier and recorder, George Collins, would be out soon to speak with me.

I left my coat in the car, and the frigid February air seemed to go right through me. I thought that I would get my coat if I had to wait outside a long time, but the Fryer soon came to the door and introduced himself. After telling him that I wanted to write about Nancy Fowler and the Conyers miracles, he directed me to "The Barn" and "The Farm" on White Road. "They will be able to tell you everything you need to know," he said, "Nancy doesn't give interviews."

When I asked him to tell me about his experiences, he laughed and said that he preferred listening to others. I realized that while I spoke with him, I became warm suddenly. The sun was beaming on my face, and I felt as warm as if it were eighty degrees outside. My face grew hot, but I didn't pay any attention to it then. After he gave me directions and returned inside the house, I walked back toward my car. I resisted the temptation to visit the Holy sights behind the house until I had more information about them.

Just as I was about to turn onto the path to the parking lot, I smelled the faint aroma of fresh roses. I also realized that the temperature was dropping fast, as if a cold draft of air was sweeping away the warmth and scent of roses.

Instantly, I was plunged into the frigid air that I had first experienced. I knew then that I had just witnessed a sign from the Holy Virgin Mary. My face and neck, where I had received two months of radiation for cancer the year before, still burned from the hot sun. I felt the burning deep in my muscles and bones. I sat in the car for almost five minutes, waiting for the burning to subside and trying to fathom what I had just experienced.

When I entered The Barn, I received a warm welcome from a friendly volunteer. She pointed to a table filled with pamphlets, books, videos, and tapes and said I could browse at my leisure. When I asked about the miracles and if they were true, she responded with an emphatic, "Yes." She gave me some pamphlets and offered to let me view one of the many videos of Nancy Fowler's visitations. When I asked her if there was a charge to see the video, she said, "No, but you're welcome to make a contribution."

The video documented reports from people who have received some kind of miracle or who have had a mystical experience. The accounts are overwhelming.

In the video an elderly woman who had been suffering from pneumonia for some months without relief from antibiotics or other medication claimed that she was cured after she drank some water from the "Holy Well."

A man who had not attended church for many years felt a power go right through him, and along with this power he experienced a profound sense of forgiveness for his sins and for not going to church.

Another gentleman who had been wheelchair-bound for several years after a stroke didn't really believe in the visitations, but he went to Conyers anyway. He was allowed into the apparition room and began to cry from a powerful emotion that came from deep with in his soul. The apparition of Mary appeared in front of her statue, and he sobbed uncontrollably. He heard a voice say to him, "Take up your cross and follow me." Afterwards, he was a changed man. All his anger about being paralyzed left him. Even though he wasn't healed physically, he had been healed emotionally. His emptiness and despair about being handicapped had left. Suddenly, he didn't care if he spent the rest of his life wheelchair-bound because he had been forgiven through God's grace, and his remorse and anger was replaced by a profound sense of peace.

Another woman said that she witnessed a golden arch over the sun and smelled the heavy scent of roses. She also saw a cross appear in the clouds.

A young woman who was shaken and moved to tears by her experience confessed that her daughter's black rosary chain had turned golden.

Jesus promised Nancy Fowler, "Gold dust will fall from Heaven. Rosaries will turn golden color, and hearts will be converted. I am healing my children. Go and believe."

Many other people have reported that the chains on their rosaries have turned golden in color. One woman reported that she had her black umbrella opened during a light mist of rain and when she closed it, it was covered with fine flakes of gold.

Another woman saw light streaming out from the heart on the Holy Mary statue. This light intensified as it covered the woman until she felt its warmth and a loving forgiveness surround her.

A younger woman saw a vision of Christ appear in front of the Holy Hill. Everyone present saw the same vision. This woman who had been away from church for 17 years, experienced a loving peace, all-forgiving and freeing.

On August 13, 1998, a crowd of visitors attended the noon prayer services, the praying of the rosary, and the stations of the cross. The prayers were almost finished when rain started to fall, and many tried to find shelter in The Barn, where books and tapes are sold. It is customary not to open the doors until the services are finished, but the women who staff The Barn knew the people were standing outside in the rain and were hoping for entrance. After a brief discussion, they decided to open the doors and immediately they received a wonderful blessing from the Holy

Mother. The entire area around the doors became filled with the heavy aroma of roses in full bloom. When the doors were opened and the crowd of people entered, the aroma of fresh roses floated over the visitors. It was as if the Holy Mother kissed each pilgrim as they were all bathed in her special scent.

As a testimony to the power of the living Jesus and the Holy Mother, these Holy signs have frequently been present at Conyers since Nancy moved there in 1990.

The sightings first began in Atlanta, Georgia, in February of 1987, when Nancy Fowler, mother of two, housewife and nurse, had reached a low point in her life. She was overcome with despair and saw only suffering and pain ahead of her. Without warning, Jesus Christ appeared before her, engulfed in a blinding supernatural light.

Nancy describes the vision: "The light was immense. It was so bright. He appeared at a time in my life when I should have been seeing the devil. I had given up all hope and was in such agony. He did not speak, but looked at me. His eyes were outstanding. They were dark and full of love, compassion, and forgiveness. My goodness, that apparition alone could have lasted me all my life."

Christ did not appear again to Nancy for nine months, but every time she prayed, a supernatural light would illuminate the crucifix in her room. During that time she also believed that she heard the voice of Our Lord giving her spiritual directions about the Universal Church. From these words of wisdom, she was getting to know Him and what caused Him pain.

On November 30, 1987, "An immense light settled over a crucifix, and Jesus appeared there in the way that is now customary, smaller in size than the first time Nancy saw Him."

She asked him,"What do You ask of me?" She wasn't surprised to receive her mission:

"To bear witness that I am the living Son of God."

Since that second appearance, Jesus has appeared to Nancy every day except for a three day period. He has been constantly available to give His love and mercy to her. Jesus has said to Nancy, "How can you bear witness that I am the living God if you can't see me all the time?" In the fall of 1990 Our Lord asked her to reveal His messages to the world.

"The cross is life. I am life. I am love. I am light. Walk from the cross, and you walk from me. Then you walk into darkness. The cross is not darkness; the cross is light. If the cross is love and life, shouldn't you want to embrace it? You are embracing me. Is there not joy in embracing Me?"

In 1987 Nancy was also experiencing apparitions of angels and the Blessed Virgin Mary.

"I heard her voice first. It was an external voice, that of a gentle woman waking me from sleep to pray. Then I was pulled by an interior call to go to Medjugorje in October 1987."

At that time Nancy was also having inner locutions.

She said, "Light would stream from the Tabernacle, and I would hear a distinct voice. Then in 1987 a dove appeared over the tabernacle, but it wasn't until 1988 that I saw the Mother of God properly.

"In the beginning, while I was in the presence of Jesus, Our Loving Mother would appear in one dimension on the wall, life size, or in the air resembling Our Lady of Fatima. Our loving mother appeared but remained silent while Her Son was appearing and speaking to me.

"Then one day I went to the chapel to pray. I opened the door, and the scent of roses flooded over me. It was overwhelming. It was then that I saw the Mother of God, life size, in a full apparition, for the first time. She was so beautiful, so radiant."

Soon after Nancy saw the first visions, she and her family suffered financial disasters and lost everything. But they never went hungry for food or emotional support. During this time of crisis, Nancy received directions from Jesus and the Holy Mother to move outside of Atlanta, away from the city lights and constant city noise. They needed a place where the whole sky could be viewed at one glance. She received a vision of what the house and grounds looked like. Nancy and a friend spent many days seeking the right location and finally discovered it in the small town of Conyers, Georgia.

Nancy lives there now with her family, close to the Holy Spirit Monastery. Fr. Joachim, a priest-monk in the Cistercian Order of the Strict Observance, has become a close friend, her confessor and spiritual adviser.

The back yard of Nancy's house slopes up a steep incline to a plateau which ends in a grove of trees. Jesus refers to the little hill as the "Holy Hill." He says people who come there to worship him will receive many graces. He is inviting everyone to come there and show faith in Him.

Jesus gave Nancy instructions on building a stone altar in the shape of a cross. This is not a standing cross, but one lying down. He said, "Build an altar in the shape of a cross. Do not be concerned what others will say. Oh, how I desire the world to be in light. I solemnly tell you, he who comes to the altar with faith, I will pour forth my graces. Oh, what gifts they will walk away with. Woe be to him who tries to destroy this cross, for I will rise up and they will be crushed to the ground. They are everyone who refuses to believe and accept my cross."

Jesus has also blessed the well that stands nearby and calls his children to use it for healing and preparation of hearts. He also asked to have a priest bless the well. Jesus has promised He will heal those who "come in faith."

When the Lord Jesus gives Nancy directions and messages to relay to the world, this testimony has become one of the greatest miracles that has ever happened in Conyers and the world. He gives these messages to the people, for the salvation of mankind and to call his people back to him.

Personal Healings at Conyers
cᴔᴔᴕ

The following healing story from Conyers is an excerpt from the book *Gifts of Grace* by Lone Jensen.

A Healing Cure

When Carmel first heard about Conyers, she knew immediately that she had to go there. Somewhere deep within her soul she felt sure she would find relief from her pain. Carmel had long been suffering from severe unremitting pain in her back and legs. The doctors advised her that her only hope of relief was immediate surgery, knee replacements for both knees. She knew their diagnosis was right because she couldn't walk without a cane for even a short distance. All the pain medication and sleeping pills she tried gave her relief for only a few hours at best.

But the idea of surgery terrified Carmel. She was over seventy years old and twenty years earlier, when she was only fifty-four, she had a terrible experience with minor surgery. At that time she had a strong premonition that she would not come out of the surgery alive. A cloud of foreboding and impending doom penetrated her every waking moment. She was so frightened that the doctor was called to reassure her, and he decided to go ahead with the surgery as soon as possible.

Carmel's heart stopped on the operating table that day and she had an out of body experience which she still remembers clearly. The doctor confessed later that he had a great deal of difficulty reviving her.

Fearing that this catastrophe would be repeated, she prayed

and prayed that somehow a miracle would occur and she wouldn't need to have the surgery on her knees.

After meeting with a group of ladies at her church, she learned about the miracles of the Holy Mother Mary and Jesus appearing at Conyers. She sensed that somehow this was an answer to her prayers. From these ladies she learned that a bus had been chartered by St. Amrose Church in Deerfield Beach, Florida, and was leaving on March 12 and returning on the 14th. She couldn't believe her luck and quickly arranged for a seat on the bus. Because the doctors had scheduled the surgery on her knees for the following week, Carmel felt sure this was a sign from the Holy Mother.

When the day arrived, Carmel awoke at five a.m. and rushed to dress and load the car. She reached the church with plenty of time to spare and waited in her car. The parking lot was deserted, and when no one arrived at seven, she decided to go into the chapel to pray for further advice. A few minutes later she felt a tap on her shoulder. A lady from the church said that they were sorry, but the trip had been canceled.

Carmel didn't know what to do. All her hopes were lost. But deep within her soul she still knew that she would find the answer to her suffering in Conyers. Her name had been chosen as one of the people to be present in the apparition room with Nancy Fowler on the thirteenth during the Virgin's visitation. The lady suggested that Carmel wait until after the seven a.m. mass was over to see if they could make other arrangements. During that mass she prayed as if her life depended on it. She prayed for someone to take her to Conyers because physically she didn't think she could drive to Georgia all alone.

After the mass she was lucky to find a woman who took her to a prayer group in Boca Raton, where the woman thought Carmel might find someone to travel with her to Conyers. The room was filled with about twenty women, all praying. After a sweet lady named Mandy introduced Carmel and told the women her story, one woman raised her hand and volunteered to drive Carmel the entire way to Conyers, Georgia, that day. Carmel couldn't believe her good fortune. Everyone in the group pitched in to help. One woman went to AAA to get maps and travel directions. Another brought sandwiches for the trip.

By one o'clock that afternoon, the ladies were on their way. It took them almost twelve hours before they arrived at Conyers. The parking lot was filled with buses and automobiles. Fortunately, Carmel had a handicapped sticker and was admitted close to the apparition room.

When they reached the apparition room, Carmel was concerned because the guides were making the people leave because the room had seating for only twenty-three people and thirty-two names were on the list. Carmel's name was among those to be in the room. She counted her admission to the room as one more of the small blessings that she had experienced on this journey.

Nancy Fowler entered the room at five minutes to twelve and knelt in front of the statue of the Virgin Mary. Carmel witnessed the Blessed Mother descend through the ceiling and float down into the statue of Our Loving Mother that was at the front of the room. A brilliant white light illuminated the entire statue, and Carmel could feel the Holy Virgin's presence and glory in that room. Tears flowed down her cheeks. Then she felt a beam of heat pierce her heart, flooding her with incredible warmth. Carmel knew immediately that she was being healed.

Carmel witnessed the Blessed Mother's presence in that room for over two hours and her ascension back to heaven, as the brilliant white light drifted upward and passed right through the ceiling. All around Carmel, in a babel of languages, people were praying their thanks for the blessing they had just received. Truly she had never experienced anything more beautiful in her life.

Carmel returned to Florida with great love and appreciation in her heart. Now she lives totally without pain, without pills,
without surgery, and she sleeps well every night.

The following year she returned to Conyers in thanksgiving to Jesus and the Blessed Mother. During that visit she decided to leave her cane—which she hasn't used since her first
visit—in testimony to her healing. Carmel's message to anyone
in pain is to have hope and faith in Jesus and the Blessed Mother,
no matter how old you are, no matter how hopeless the situation.

THE BLEEDING STATUE OF JESUS

MFH Graphics

The Miraculous Sign in Bolivia

On October 13, 1995, Nancy Fowler received a message from Jesus: "I have created many witnesses. Let them go out and speak."

On March 7, 1996, Nancy visited the country of Bolivia to speak about her visions. Not long before she was to give her talk, she was meditating in a private room when Jesus appeared to her. He told her that he would leave another sign of his presence in Bolivia. She felt this message to be very true and so she spoke of it in her talk. On March 9, after finishing her mission, she returned to Atlanta, Georgia.

At six p.m. that same day a woman who lived in the city of Cochabamba, Bolivia, bought a beautiful statue of Jesus. She took it home and realized immediately that the statue began to cry. She later learned that this occurred at approximately the same time that Nancy's plane was arriving in Atlanta.

The statue continued to cry and small drops of blood appeared on its forehead where the crown of thorns penetrated Christ's skin. On the 22nd of April, the owner of the statue decided to visit Nancy in Georgia to talk about the bleeding statue of Jesus and what this meant.

Nancy wasn't feeling well, so she asked the lady to come into her bedroom where she was lying down on her bed. When the lady came into the room, she sat down and began to tell Nancy the story about her statue that was bleeding real drops of blood and crying real tears. The woman was very surprised to see the same statue that she had bought on the ninth of March sitting in Nancy's room. When she told Nancy of this coincidence, Nancy replied, "This is the only statue I have here in my room. I like it. I prefer this one."

The statue has been studied and samples of the "blood"

were taken and analyzed in two labs, one in New Orleans and the other in Australia. The results were conclusive; the drainage on the face of the statue was human blood. But something else was found with the blood, and when it was analyzed they discovered it to be a piece of a real thorn.

Last September 29, after seven months of study, the Church authorities in Bolivia recognized this phenomena as authentic. The Bishop and the Catholic Archdiocese have given the rules and permissions for the Catholics to pray at this statue and the authorization to build a chapel in the name of Christ.

The Miracle of the Stigmata

Catalina came on a pilgrimage to Conyers for the October 13, 1994, anniversary apparition. She knelt before the life-size statue of the crucifix of Christ on the Holy Hill.

Catalina related her experience:

"I saw a light all around the Christ, a very strong light. And then I saw the necessity to offer my life to the Lord, so that He could use it in whatever way He needed to use it, to give thanks for all that He did for me.

"Then I closed my eyes and I stayed praying, and when I opened them, two very strong lights came out of the hands of my Lord and I felt like a lightning bolt had gone through my own hands. I felt the strong pain, and then a light came out of His feet, and it came to my own feet. The light split in two toward my own two feet. The third light came out of His side, it went straight to my heart, and there I fell to the ground because the pain was too strong.

"The following Friday, when we were in Costa Rica, there the Lord told me: 'Enjoy the gift that I have given you in Conyers because there are many people that ask Me for this to share the suffering of My Cross—and this I reserve only for those that are capable to love Me as I need to be loved.'"

"Then I asked Him. It (the stigmata) should not be seen ever?"

"And He told me: 'For now, no. But, when I think it is necessary, this can be seen by all. . .'"

After this vision at the cross of Jesus, Catalina passed out, and the emergency ambulance was called to take her to the hospital. Ever since that day, every first Friday of the month she experiences the pain, suffering, and stigmata (wounds in her hands, hip and feet) that Jesus Christ experienced when he was crucified on the cross.

It always begins the same. Jesus says, "Can you help me today?" And she answers, "Yes, I will."

The stigmata usually begins around noon on the first Friday of the month. Small wounds bearing tiny spots of blood appear on her forehead, as if she were wearing the crown of thorns. She doesn't feel well and needs to lie down. About 20 minutes later, blood is dripping down her forehead and wounds have opened on her palms and feet on both sides. She suffers as a person who is dying because she can't get any air, as Christ suffered when he hung on the cross. She is in agony until about 3:00 p.m. when the symptoms begin to subside. By 8:00 p.m. that evening she is up walking around and feeling fine, completely relieved of her symptoms. But large wounds are still present on her feet, hands and side. By the next morning they have disappeared without a trace.

Since her first vision, Catalina has become a visionary like Nancy and also receives direction from Jesus about the salvation of the world. Many who visit Conyers become disciples of Jesus Christ. Many pilgrims return home spiritually renewed and tell their friends and church the wonderful miracles that are occurring in Conyers and the messages that the Living Jesus is revealing.

More Healings at Conyers

Maria has visited the Conyers religious site as many as twelve or thirteen times on the thirteenth day of the month. The first time she took her son who was around nine-or ten-years-old. She was worried that he wouldn't be able to sit still through the two hours of prayers and speakers, so she brought a big bag filled with cars, trucks, puzzles, and books to entertain him. He was usually hyperactive and busy all the time, but she wanted him to have the experience of going to Conyers anyway.

Right away, Maria noticed a strange thing happening. From the moment she arrived at the religious site and settled into her seat, Nick sat quietly on the ground and didn't move. He prayed when she did, and he never seemed in the least bit restless. He prayed the rosary for two hours or more and never asked for any toys or even made a peep. She couldn't believe how quiet he was. She had never seen him that calm before.

All around them people were taking pictures of the sky and clouds trying to capture the Virgin Mary on film, but they never saw anything. Maria used her camera which developed pictures instantly. Nick asked if he could take a picture of the sun, too. She didn't want to let him, thinking that the film would be ruined; but she gave in because he had been so good.

When Nick's pictures developed, she and her friends watched as the unique images appeared in the bright glow of the sun. When they looked into the sun, they couldn't see anything that resembled the photographs. One special picture showed an open door and stairs coming out of the sun. The faint white image of a woman wearing a long flowing dress, possibly the Virgin Mary, stood on the stairs. (see cover)

Other people gathered around them and were so excited about the pictures that they asked Nick if he would use their cameras to take pictures. Similar images appeared in these photographs too. Maria used her own camera to take a picture again, but the only thing that appeared in the photo was the exact cloud formation that they were seeing. In all fifteen pictures that Nick took, the open door was visible. Maria thinks that Nick was given the gift of a seer when using the cameras.

Later that morning, Nick remarked to his mother while he was praying the rosary, "Mama, the wind is petting my hair." But when she looked around, there was no wind or even a faint breeze. She thought it was the Holy Spirit who was patting his head.

After that day Nick no longer seemed hyperactive. He was just as calm as his mother or other normal children. Maria and her family were so grateful that they prayed every day for thanksgiving to the Blessed Mother. Nick also performed much better in school. Maria thought the change in her son was a miracle.

The Pictures

Jesus's message from Conyers is, "I am the Living Son of God. Come here and receive a blessing from me."

The photographs of the open door in the sky seem to echo Jesus's message. They are a direct invitation from God to see his power and blessings. In the Bible whenever a passage mentions a door or window opening into heaven usually miraculous graces follow. The following verses are samples of this image.

Malachi 3:10: Bring all the tithes into the storehouse, that there may be (food) in my house, and test me now herewith, saith the Lord of hosts, if I will not open for you the windows of heaven, and pour out for you a blessing, that there shall not be room enough to receive it.

Psalms 78:23: Though he had commanded the clouds from above and opened the doors of heaven, and had rained down manna upon them to eat and had given them of the grain of heaven... .

Job 38:17: Hast the gates of death been revealed unto thee? Or hast thou seen the doors of the shadow of death?

Revelation 3:8: I know thy works; behold I set before the an open door, and no man can shut it; for thou hast little strength and hast kept my word and hast not denied my name.

Revelation 3:20: Behold, I stand at the door and knock; if any man hear my voice, and open the door, I will come in to him, and will sup with him, and be with him.

Revelation 4:1: After this I looked and behold, a door was opened in heaven; and the first voice that I heard was , as it were, of a trumpet talking with me; which said, Come up here, and I will show thee things which must be hereafter.

John 10:9: I am the door; by me if any man enter in, he shall be saved, and shall go in and out, and find pasture.

Acts 14:27: And when they had come and had gathered the church together, they reviewed all that God had done with them, and how he had opened the door of faith unto the Gentiles.

Do the following pictures show us the doors into the third heaven, God's paradise?

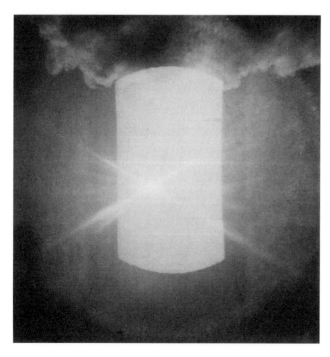

PICTURES FROM CONYERS, GEORGIA

Taken by Nick Thompson

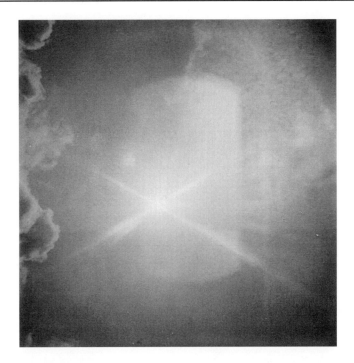

PICTURES FROM CONYERS, GEORGIA

Taken by Nick Thompson

PICTURES FROM CONYERS, GEORGIA

Taken by Nick Thompson

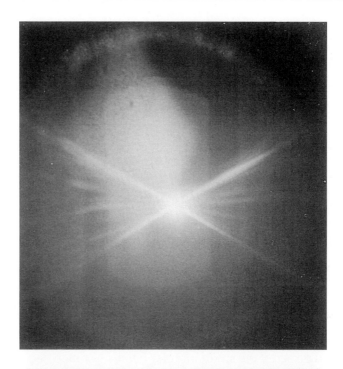

PICTURES FROM CONYERS, GEORGIA

Taken by Nick Thompson

Are these pictures the doors that enter the Third Heaven mentioned in 2 Corinthians 12:2. I knew a man in Christ above fourteen years ago...– such a one caught up to the third heaven. In the concordance the "third heaven" was described as the abode of God, the first heaven being that of the clouds, and the second heaven that of the stars.

A Bounty of Light

On another occasion, Maria arrived at The Farm in Conyers early and waited with thousands of people outside on the lawn for Nancy Fowler, the visionary, to appear. Maria remembers that five minutes before the service, everyone suddenly had spots of lights glowing all over their bodies, as if the visitors held flashlights and directed the small circular beams to touch each person around them or a strobe light.

But not one person revealed a flashlight and everyone "oohed and aahed" at the sight. The experience was similar to attending a circus or a sporting event where people are flashing the brilliant rays from their flashlights all around the room. Maria thinks it was another miracle.

Taking His Will

Around the same time Maria started to go to Conyers regularly, a spot on her lung was discovered during a routine chest x-ray. After she went to St. Joseph's Hospital in Atlanta for a second opinion, the surgeon informed her that the spot looked malignant. The doctor told her that she needed a biopsy as soon as possible. Nick, her son, was very small, and she was so upset about the diagnosis that she didn't know what to do. She didn't want to die and leave her son motherless.

On the way home to Milledgeville, Georgia, Maria stopped at the Catholic Monastery in Conyers to pray. A nun came up to her and asked if she could help. Maria told the nun about the diagnosis of cancer and how upset she was. The nun told Maria to pray and to tell Jesus that she was leaving her will with Him and taking His will. When Maria left, the nun said she would pray for Maria's recovery.

Two days later, Maria returned to St. Joseph Hospital in Atlanta for the biopsy of the spot on the lung. The nurse put the IV in her arm and then took her to the x-ray department for a CAT Scan. Two scans were done and then Maria was brought back to the outpatient surgery area. The nurse removed the IV and told her the biopsy wasn't needed. The spot that was thought to be malignant turned out to be a harmless calcified area.

Maria attributes her good fortune to the powerful healing touch of God. She has been thankful ever since and tries to attend the services in Conyers whenever she can. She is a devout Catholic and prays the rosary every day.

Maria and Nick feel as if these photographs were a gift from Jesus to let people know that His Spirit is here on earth. They show the pictures to everyone they can and hope to inspire others the way they have been inspired.

Maria Thompson
Nick Thompson
Milledgeville, Georgia

The Last Visit
ఴఀఀఄ

On October 13, 1998, Conyers, Georgia, was besieged again by bumper to bumper traffic jams; cars and busses from as far away as Texas, New Mexico, Michigan, New York and Louisiana, to name a few, were filled with religious pilgrims who wanted to witness the appearance of the Virgin Mary for the last time. Old women walking with canes, young mothers pushing strollers, men carrying coolers and toddlers all crowded along the grass paths that led to the religious site. Eventually the numbers totaled more than one hundred thousand, a record for the eight years that the visionary Nancy Fowler has witnessed the divine appearance of Jesus and the Virgin Mary.

The crowds were not disappointed. Reports of miraculous sightings began the evening of the twelfth when visitors from New York waiting for their bus to receive gas at a local station realized that something was happening with the sun. The huge red ball was just about to set and one woman yelled out, "Look at the sun."

It was spinning in the sky. The pilgrims poured out of the bus and fell to their knees, crying and praying at the sight of the sun actually spinning in the sky.

One observer, Renzo Garcia, said that there was a white cloud line marking the sky and the sun seemed to be bouncing up and down across that line. At the same time as it was spinning in its orbit, the sun changed colors, and at one time turned a dazzling yellow, then blue.

Another woman, Linda Taverax, also from New York, saw the Eucharist inside the sun, and beside this she saw the Crucifix.

Someone next to her saw a loaf of bread breaking and one small piece fell to the earth.

Several other visitors, who had arrived at the site early that evening and were placing their chairs for the next day, saw the same spinning sun.

The next day on the thirteenth, thousands arrived early to wait for the visionary to begin at noon. There were so many people that it took several hours from the time they reached the town of Conyers until they parked and found a place to sit, a task that ordinarily would take only five or ten minutes. Not one person seemed irritable because of the traffic. They were all so excited to be there.

People of all walks of life and many different languages seemed to be speaking at the same time, each telling their tales of previous visits. One man was showing pictures taken by Aquilina Arenas from North Charleston, South Carolina, of other visits to Conyers. One picture taken in the parking lot at 9:30 a.m. on February 13, 1994, of the sun breaking through the clouds revealed an image of the Virgin Mary dressed in a white cape. Her brown hair was showing out of the hood and her lovely, fine-featured face was visible. Beside the Virgin in the upper right corner was a cloud in the form of an angel blowing a trumpet.

Another picture taken on February 7, 1994, by Aquilina shortly after sunrise displayed a giant white cross in the sky. Beside this in another cloud formation was another angel.

Another picture that they took at night at the holy site showed the apparition of a white rosary. These pictures were all instantly developed.

Another woman named Anna Mae Charpentier from Louisiana said that when she visited the site in 1994, she saw the image of the Virgin Mary descend from the sky over the apparition building. She and her family saw the image when Nancy

Fowler said that the Virgin is coming.

In 1998 while the pilgrims were waiting for the services to start, Anna Mae's husband, Steven, pulled out the page of directions to read for the rosary. He realized that he had forgotten his glasses and couldn't read the text. But only a few minutes had elapsed when he confessed that he could now see the letters clearly and read each word without his glasses. This was the first time in thirty years that he could do this.

At 12:00 noon the blue sky was completely free of clouds. Several minutes after twelve, just as the services began, the white edge of a cloud seemed to fall out from under the sun. Then puffs of smoke colored clouds spewed out from each side of the sun on the right and on the left at the same time. It resembled the power of God in the sky pictured in the movie *The Ten Commandments*. Within seconds the sun began to spin and pulled in behind it the dark clouds which seemed to surround the sun in an orbit formation and dimmed the brilliant rays. The sun kept spinning very fast, resembling a top, and turned several colors, first blue, then teal edged with black, then yellow with a dazzling yellow light surrounding the cloud. At that time the yellow light fell straight to the ground as if in a column from the sun to the earth. Then a yellow glowing light covered everything around. It was as if we were looking through yellow plastic. The temperature even cooled to this florescent type of light. Some people were covered in yellow spots. At first we thought this was from the bright light in our eyes, but when we moved our eyes the spots stayed stationary. Then just as instantly as it all started, the sun returned to its orbit and radiated out its light as if nothing had ever happened.

Many people were taking instant pictures which revealed the doors into the heavens. Some even showed the images of angels. Seeing thousands of people praying their rosary beads and thanking God for such a wonderful display was a powerfully and thanking God for such a wonderful display was a powerfully inspirational sight. The feeling of love prevailed throughout the crowd and people were sharing their miracle experiences.

Nancy Fowler saw the Virgin Mary that day for the last time until she reaches heaven. The Virgin asked that a church be built on the site in honor of the visitations. Nancy saw a vision of the completed building with the Virgin Mary kneeling on the roof. Later in the apparition room the Virgin Mary said that as a gift of grace for all the visitors she would free many souls from purgatory into heaven. She asked that we pray for peace and reconciliation in the world, and love each other.

Many souls were saved that day, but there was a sadness that prevailed because this would be the last time the Virgin Mary would come to Conyers. Many had returned repeatedly over the years and gained spiritual strength from their visits. For some this pilgrimage has been the highlight of their year. But they can still find hope and strength in the knowledge that Jesus Christ is the living Son of God and we can find him everywhere.

Bibliography

Jensen, Lone. *Gifts of Grace*. New York, NY., HarperCollins
    Publishers, Inc., 1995.

Our Loving Mother's Children. *Journal of Reported Teachings
    And Messages of Our Lord and Our Loving Mother at
    Conyers, Georgia, USA*. Our Loving Mother's Children,
    Conyers, Georgia.

Our Loving Mother's Children. *To Bear Witness that I AM the
    LIVING SON of GOD*. Our Loving Mother's Children,
    Conyers, Georgia.

For more information about Conyers, please write: Our
Loving Mother's Children, P.O. Box 309, Conyers, Georgia
30207.

All messages from the Holy Mother can be obtained from
their web site: www.conyers.org; or our Loving Mother's Children.

Many of the stories included here are first person testimo-
nials given by special permission for use in this book.

‹◦◦›
Personal
Miracle
Stories
‹◦◦›

The Mysterious Brick Wall
୧ᢙᡠᡄᢅᢍ

After returning home from shopping one rainy night in 1995, when Edna opened the front door to her house, she immediately sensed that something strange was going on, but she couldn't identify the cause of her feelings. She was usually a very practical person and not moved by small incidents, so she acknowledged these feelings and entered the hall slowly and cautiously. She heard a clamor coming from the kitchen which sounded like dishes and pans being moved around, but thought her son was in there getting something to eat.

Edna tried to squelch her worries and headed toward the telephone table and chair where she always put her handbag and packages after shopping, but this time, she ran into an invisible wall that felt as strong and solid as if it were brick. She couldn't reach the chair or table in the hall even though she repeatedly tried to force her way through the barrier. Perplexed and confused by the situation, she stood there for only a few seconds when a whisper of a voice said, "Go into the Bathroom. You'll be safe there." She followed the directions as quickly as she could, although she felt a little foolish.

Almost ten minutes later, she decided to leave the bathroom. When she returned to the hall, this time she easily placed her packages on the table. There was no obstacle, no wall. When she reached the kitchen, she saw the back door standing open. She ran to her son's room wondering if he was in there. His bedroom door stood open too, the lock smashed, and his gun, which usually hung on the wall, was missing. Later, she found out that he was still at work.

She knew then why the voice directed her into the bath-room. The voice that came to her that rainy evening probably saved her life. Evidently the robber got away without knowing that she had entered the home.

This is the first premonition or supernatural experience that Edna has ever had. She still remembers the message, "Go into the bathroom..." as if it just happened, it sounded so realistic.

Every Sunday, all her life, Edna has attended church and loved her religious home. But in all those years, she has never experienced supernatural phenomena. This incident has made her realize that God is real and that his angels are watching over her. Her whole life has changed. Before when people told her their personal experiences, she didn't really believe them. She doesn't know why she didn't. She always thought the tales in the Bible were lovely stories that happened hundreds of years ago. It never occurred to her that they might be true.

"Now, I truly believe that God is real," she said. "Before, I always had little doubts."

Edna Brown
Macon, Georgia

Miracle at Oconee River

Barbara had spent a lovely Sunday visiting with close friends in Sandersville, Georgia. They had been friends for years and were celebrating a family reunion. This was the first time they had seen each other since her husband's funeral two years before. When she got up to leave, she realized that the time had slipped away from her, and it was past nine-thirty. She wouldn't arrive home in Macon until eleven, and she hated to drive the country roads that late at night.

She hurriedly said her good-byes and rushed to her car, telling her friends not to worry, she'd be all right. But she hadn't been in the car for more than twenty minutes when she felt herself nod off. She awoke just in time to prevent the car from swerving off the road and swore to herself that this wouldn't happen again. She felt relieved that a serious accident had been avoided.

Barbara saw the Milledgeville lights in the distance and relaxed, knowing she would be passing through a town with brightly lit streets. But when she approached the Oconee River, she dozed off again. Only this time she didn't wake herself.

Through the black fog of sleep, she heard the words, "Mama," spoken loudly and sternly in a very familiar voice— that of her beloved dead husband. She woke up with a start, just in time to see his form standing on the side of the Oconee River bridge and just in time to veer away from crashing her car over the concrete railing.

Her husband had been dead for two long, painful years. That night his spirit came to her to save her life. She knows this in her heart. She will never forget the expression of worry on his face. It was the same old look that she had seen many times, especially when their life had taken a tragic turn. She believes that his spirit is with her still and is looking out for her. His presence that night has brought her great comfort.

Barbara J. Skipper

The Angel in the Marble
cↃ⊙☉ↄ

The Marble Angel

Nancy and her daughter have been members of the First United Methodist Church in Tucker, Georgia, for years. One day when a group of people were praying in the chapel, they discovered the image of a beautiful angel in the marble wall behind the cross. The image is outlined by the natural graining of the stones. Although no one knows how, four squares come together to form the image of the angel. The angel is just to the right of the beautiful brass cross. The chapel was originally built in 1941, but in 1971 when the chapel was remodeled, the marble was added to the wall behind the altar.

The parishioners are sure the image is the work of an angel and has always been there. It has just recently been brought to their attention. They believe that it is a small miracle from God.

Amazing Aunt Grace

Aunt Grace celebrated her eighty-eighth birthday in a nursing home in Greensboro, North Carolina. All her life she was called amazing by her family because she was so full of enthusiasm and did outlandish things. Over the past few years she has become very depressed and grumpy about everything. The food wasn't good. She couldn't get around very well anymore. Her roommates were too noisy. Nothing anyone did for her ever pleased her.

One afternoon as Grace lay resting in her bed, she glanced across the room, and a life-size angel appeared to her. The angel wore a beautiful flowing white dress, but the features on her face were too fuzzy to see every detail. Large white wings stood out clearly behind the angel, although the delicate edges of the feathers were blurry. Aunt Grace was sure she had seen a live angel. Immediately, she called all her family members and told them the news. She couldn't talk about anything else for weeks.

From that moment on Aunt Grace was a changed person. Her old, optimistic self returned, and she was happy all the time. She didn't complain about anything; in fact, everything pleased her. The food was great. Her roommate was wonderful, and her own many ailments were finally tolerable. The appearance of the supernatural image gave Aunt Grace hope that there was life after life, something she had not fully believed before.

Nancy Page
Eatonton, Georgia

THE VIRGIN MARY

Picture by Judy Wheeler

The Virgin Mary
ed℗℗v

Clearwater, Florida

A beautiful outline of the Virgin Mary appeared on the glass face of an office building on the corner of US 19 and Drew Street in Clearwater, Florida, in December of 1996. Several weeks before Christmas nine mirror panels of copper-tinted glass were miraculously transformed by some force, either chemical or mystical to reflect the iridescent rainbow shape of the Virgin Mary.

"God is giving us a sign," said Sister Martin, a nun of the order of St. Anne in Bangalore, India.

Some people say the image has been on the glass since 1994 and just became visible to the public after a large tree was removed. Others say that it appeared after sudsy water splattered on the mirror-covered building from a car wash across the street.

Others speculate about the cause, but no one has been able to completely explain how a 60 x 20 foot image of the Virgin Mary appeared on the side of the glass building.

One witness challenged the others by saying, "If the cause of the image was the sudsy mist of water coming from the car wash across the street, then why wasn't the image of a car or truck or even just a splash present on the side of the building. There must be some supernatural meaning behind the presence of the Virgin Mary."

Over a million pilgrims have visited the site searching for inspiration and meaning to their lives. She is not a woody version of the icon, but a gentle silhouette of the Blessed Lady, whose head is lovingly tilted toward the crowds. Perhaps this vision gives us clear evidence that the Virgin Mary's spirit is alive and well after all, watching over us in our daily circle of life. No one can tell for sure, but thousands of people are visiting the site every month, so many that the Clearwater Police Department had to increase their budget $40,000 a year to handle the crowds. The building has changed hands several times and is now owned by the Ugly Duckling Car Sales and used for their offices. I suppose that this is great advertising for them.

Judy Wheeler

A Grandfather's Approval

Leila Stone had always been a good Christian and loved the Lord. During a prayer meeting at church one night, the minister shouted, "He's calling you. Come up before the Lord and receive your bounty. Accept the Lord into your heart. Come up here tonight." Leila felt this invitation as a personal call for her life. This call touched her deeper than anything she had ever experienced before.

During all the other prayer meetings, she considered herself already saved. This time was different. An invisible force seemed to be carrying her forward as she walked up to the altar. When the minister's hand rested on her head, she felt the power of God go right through her from her head to her toes. Afterwards, when the room swayed back and forth a little and she had trouble walking back to the pew, she knew that the power of the Holy Spirit had penetrated her body. For the rest of the evening she was thrilled that she had made the decision to go forward.

That night her grandfather's spirit came to her in a dream. He didn't say anything to her. But the visit by his spirit was so real that it gives her chills when she talks about it. That night he communicated to her his tremendous joy that she had taken this important step. His excitement over her commitment to God seemed to infiltrate her mind. It was as if he were standing beside her, but no one was present in her room.

She still wonders how his spirit could communicate his feelings to her because she firmly believes that he is in heaven. But she thinks that his spirit must be her guardian angel and feels as if he is looking after her. This feeling that she received from him has been an important life force and helps bring the scriptures alive for her. She believes without a doubt that his spirit is in heaven because during his life he was such a devout man. She wants to follow in his footsteps.

Leila Stone
High Falls, Georgia

Pushed by an Angel
ఆఁఄఀ

All her life Julia has been sensitive to the supernatural. Whenever she visits historic landmarks, spirits appear before her. Once she visited the Civil War battle field of Chickamauga, and when she walked out of the pavilion, she saw the silent images of the Confederate army pass before her. They were wounded, angry men, giant cannons pulled by horses, and officers sitting high on their mounts shouting silent orders to their regiments. It felt as if she had been transposed for a second into the 1860s. Then after the passing of another few seconds, she was looking out onto the deserted fields of grass. When she spoke with the park ranger later, he verified that quite a few people had seen similar activity in that same spot over the years.

Her husband doesn't understand her sightings and denies their existence. He doesn't want her to talk about them either. She believes that he doesn't want people to think that she is strange. To her, though, these occurrences seem just normal.

Julia first experienced the supernatural when she was a tiny five-year-old. She raced across the street to get away from her older brother who tormented her all the time. But in her fury of escaping his grasp, she didn't see the silver grill of the eighteen-wheeler truck speeding towards her. Just as it was about to crush her little body under its immense wheels, she felt a fierce blast of air and a hand push her so hard that she flew through the air. She landed standing upright on the sidewalk on the opposite side of the street. It was as if someone had picked her up and gently set her down on the concrete. Not realizing how much danger she had been in, she remembers being filled with rage. She thought that the push came from her brother. As she glanced up, the wind from the passing semi nearly knocked her over. When the dust cleared, she saw the stone-white face of her brother who was still standing on the curb on the other side of the street. He stared at her live body in disbelief. A chill went through her small frame when she realized that an angel must have saved her life. As long as she lives, she will never forget that look of terror on her brother's face.

Ever since that day, Julia knew that she had been saved from a terrible death for a special reason. She still remembers feeling that angel's hand pressing on her back. All these years she has been very sensitive to the spirit world. But this has been a lonely experience for her. Few people believe her stories. She has learned to keep her visions and sightings to herself. Sometimes she gets premonitions that are so powerful and life threatening she can't forget about them. She tries to intervene the best way she can without letting the person know that she has actually had a premonition concerning their future.

When Julia confides in her daughter about the experiences, her daughter doesn't want to listen or have anything to do with the stories. Julia realizes that her family doesn't understand her ability and has stopped talking about it. She has been given a rare gift to be able to see into the other side of life. She is a productive person with a good job, and not taking medication.

Many people suffer with their spiritual gifts because most people don't believe them and even persecute them for their ability. The Saints were persecuted this way, too, and had to remove themselves from the public, but they never denied their visions. God gave them the strength to withstand the criticism and ridicule.

Saved from Night Terrors
⋰⊙⊙⋱

When Sylvia was a young child she suffered from terrible nightmares and woke up crying in the middle of the night, riddled with fear after seeing terrible visions in her dreams. The experiences were so real that she carried the fear with her all during the next day. As she grew older, she was able to deal with the fear, telling herself that the scares would never actually happen, that they were just dreams. But the night terrors never stopped. She was plagued with her disturbed sleep even into adulthood.

Sylvia's mother also endured a lifetime of disturbing, terror-filled dreams and sympathized with her daughter's plight. Unfortunately, all the sympathy in the world didn't fend off the demons of the night.

At a prayer service at church one night, Sylvia received a personal call from Jesus and went forward to acknowledge that Jesus was her Lord and Savior and to claim his gift of love and forgiveness. She was saved that night along with several others. She didn't feel any different right away, but a few days later she realized that her disturbing nightly visions had vanished.

A few nights later Sylvia woke up and saw the figure of Jesus standing at the foot of her bed.

He said only a few words, "My peace I give. My peace I bring." She was overwhelmed by a tremendous feeling of love and forgiveness. Then He disappeared.

Ever since that night, she has been completely free from nightmares. In that moment, her life changed, and from then on she has been active in her church and loves the Lord. She didn't realize that life could be so wonderful and free from worry. She thanks the Lord every day for His powerful intervention in her life.

Sylvia Moss

Red Veronica

Gloria, Jenny Hatfield's niece, remembers her Aunt Jenny as being the kindest person that she has ever known. Gloria remembers seeing the red veronica plant growing almost as large as a bush in the middle of her aunt's backyard. For as far back as Gloria can remember her mother told her this wonderful story of her Aunt Jenny and the origin of the red veronica plant.

One spring evening in the 1930s, Jenny Hatfield was washing her dinner dishes at the hand pump on her back porch in Georgia. Many of the homes in rural Georgia during those years, like hers, didn't have inside plumbing. Just as she was pumping enough water to wash another pan full of dishes, she gazed out at her yard and the meadow beyond. In an instant and without warning the life-size figure of Jesus appeared to her. He stood full bodied in the middle of her back yard. She was so overwhelmed that she walked down the steps and out into the yard, never taking her eyes off of him, and never saying a word. She wanted to touch Him to make sure she wasn't dreaming.

She looked up into his peaceful eyes and said, "You're real."

He answered, "Yes, I am."

"Why would you come to visit someone like me?" Jenny asked, thinking that she wasn't worthy of a visit from Jesus, the Son of God.

He said that He had come to her personally because she believed and loved Him so much. He wanted her to go to everyone she knew and tell them how much she loved Him, and how much He loved everyone on earth.

The day after Jenny saw Jesus standing in her back yard, a circle of red veronica grew up in the place where He had stood. It grew there every summer for as long as Jenny Hatfield lived in that house, and Jenny followed Jesus's directions and professed God's love to all she knew and met until the day she died.

Gloria Fowler

A Gift of Life
~∾⟳∽~

One a rainy afternoon about twenty years ago a terrible collision occurred between a tiny Volkswagen and a large stationwagon, leaving three dead and Roger, the driver of the Volkswagen, severely injured. Roger suffered multiple fractures all over his body, including both femurs and several ribs, which compromised his breathing. When he reached the hospital emergency room, the doctors and nurses concentrated all their energies on trying to save his life. After spending several days in the intensive care unit, it looked like he would be all right. But he still needed extensive surgery on both legs and his hip. The doctor was terribly concerned about whether or not Roger would ever walk again.

After a few weeks of recovery, Roger underwent surgery to place a long rod in his femur to strengthen the bone enough to hold weight. The 25-year-old boy was still in danger of not being able to walk because his other leg needed more surgery, too. Roger was thankful to be alive and endured the endless pain and suffering, hoping that in the end he would be able to walk like a normal person.

Several weeks later, Dr. Pedro Tamayo took Roger back to surgery to place a pin in his other femur and pelvis. He tolerated the anesthesia well, and just as Dr. Tamayo was about to place the pin into position, Roger's heart stopped. Without warning, the pulse line on the monitor became flat. Buzzers went off and Dr. Tamayo began resuscitation with heart massage, CPR. When the hospital heard of the emergency in the OR, several other doctors came in to help. They began a cut-down in the arm to start a central line for all the medications needed to be given. One doctor helped Dr. Tamayo with the resuscitation. Precious seconds passed and turned into minutes and still no heart beat appeared. Several minutes had passed before the doctors began to question if it was time to stop or not. They feared that sufficient time had passed for brain damage to occur.

Dr. Tamayo persisted knowing that many minutes had passed and that the brain became severely damaged when deprived of oxygen and blood, he prayed silently, "Please God, in your infinite wisdom and mercy, give this boy another chance. He is so young . . . with his entire life ahead of him. Please find it in your heart to bring him back to life. I don't ask this for myself, but for this young man's family and friends. He has been such a fine person."

The other doctors were saying, "Come on Pedro. It's time to give up." They were trying to help him out by making the decision for him. But he just kept on breathing and praying. Suddenly, the blip of a heartbeat appeared on the screen, and another, and another, and another, until a stable rhythm flashed across the monitor. Dr. Tamayo was overcome with emotion and immediately thanked God. "What a wonderful gift. What a wonderful gift God has given this boy, his family, and me," Pedro said later.

The other doctors were also amazed, but still dubious about the outcome, fearing brain damage in the patient. Dr. Tamayo decided to close the surgery and finish the leg's healing with traction. He told the family right away what had happened, and they were all thankful for the miracle. Weeks later, everyone was even more thankful when a complete evaluation proved no brain damage whatsoever had occurred.

Almost thirty years later, Dr. Tamayo still receives a Christmas card from Roger just as he has every year since the accident. Dr. Tamayo has never forgotten that the Lord took pity on this boy and gave him another chance at life. He has never forgotten that miracles are possible and he is still thankful for the experience of seeing this happen. It has deeply touched his life.

Dr. Pedro Tamayo
Milledgeville, Georgia

Peggy's Dream
cᘐᕲᕲᘐ

Peggy was a heavy abuser of alcohol and had been for many years, but the time had come when she was in danger of losing her job and everything she owned. Her daughter was at the point of wanting to commit her to the state mental hospital in Milledgeville, Georgia.

Peggy knew she had been a burden to her family for more than thirty years. And for many of these years her daughter had threatened to "put her away." But this time seemed to be the worst and her last chance. She knew that she had finally hit rock bottom. All her promises fell on deaf ears. Seeing no hope for the future, she contemplated suicide. She saw only two choices for her life, suicide or alcohol rehabilitation. Each choice was just as difficult and painful as the other because she had never been able to control her obsession and desire for alcohol.

Before Peggy fell asleep, she prayed to Jesus and asked if He could help her although she felt she couldn't blame Him if He refused. Through tears of pain, she admitted to God that she was a poor, miserable sinner.

That night while asleep, she dreamed she was sitting at a table looking out a window at fields of wheat ready for harvest. The golden wheat fields were so vast that they covered the earth as far as she could see until they disappeared into the horizon. She saw herself sitting in her kitchen at the table, but she resembled her grandmother, an old and wrinkled woman. Thousands of shimmering, golden heads of wheat were swaying in the soft summer breeze, and a peaceful feeling came over her. It was so forgiving and loving that it showed her how replenishing true love could be.

When she awoke the next morning, she felt the unconditional love that she had felt in her dream. In her peace she was so thankful for the experience that she knelt down and thanked God for that wonderful feeling.

Peggy didn't realize exactly what had happened to her then, but later she knew that she had become a new person. The old Peggy was dead, and the new Peggy no longer desired alcohol in any form. She experienced a miracle and gives all the credit to Jesus. She hasn't had a drink of alcohol since. She believes in the power of God here and now and has never forgotten the experience even though it occurred more than twenty years ago. Every day she thanks Jesus for coming into her life and saving her from certain ruin.

"Jesus healed me!" she often tells other people who suffer from alcohol dependence at rehabilitation groups. "And I have never been happier. He can heal you, too. You can count on it."

Peggy is always hopeful when speaking to large groups and believes that if even one person is helped, her time is well spent. But few people think her story has anything to do with them. They have difficulty in believing in miracles. They have even more difficulty in believing that a miracle can happen to them.

Peggy continues to share her story because she believes that if she can recieve a miracle, others can too. There was a time when she felt she wasn't worth saving, but Jesus touched her life and brought a miracle at her worst moment. She says, "All you have to do is pray and ask for his help. Believe me, he'll be there in a second."

A Simple Prayer
୧ඁ

Gene woke up one morning with a stiffness in his neck that he expected to go away in a day or two. But as time went on, he was barely able to move his neck. With the rigidity came pain, especially in the area where his neck met his body. When the pain grew too much for him, he finally gave in and decided to go to the doctor even though he was a man who always prided himself for having a high tolerance for pain and seldom needed a doctor. His family doctor said he thought this condition was rather serious requiring a specialist and referred Gene to a neurologist. During the time between appointments, the pain grew even more intolerable.

The neurologist showed Gene the x-ray of his entire spine and pointed to the place where the pain originated. The doctor shook his head with disappointment, saying, "This is your problem here. It doesn't look good. This tiny point of bone is a spur that is pressing on your spine and causing the excruciating pain you are suffering. Surgery will be so dangerous that you might be better off enduring the pain, but either way you will probably suffer for the rest of your life."

Gene could see the tiny spur where the doctor's finger rested on the x-ray. By this time Gene's neck movement was limited and he couldn't move his head from one side to the other without moving his entire upper body, so the news devastated him. He saw himself as a pain invalid for the rest of his life, dependent on strong medications for comfort. He thought that there must be some way he might overcome this dilemma. The pain was too great to stand even for a short time, much less for years.

For months, Gene tolerated his life by taking strong pain relievers, wanting to live his life the best way he could, especially for his family, but he saw his future flash clearly before him and didn't know how he could cope.

A year had passed since Gene received the diagnosis of a spinal bone spur, when he visited his neighborhood Methodist Church one evening for services. One of the ushers came up to him and announced that a healing service was about to start. A friend suggested that maybe he would find some relief from his pain if he went up to the altar to receive a healing by the evangelist.

Gene having suffered with neck and back pain for so long, thought for a second, prayed for a few moments, and then decided to go up when the time was right. But while he was sitting in the congregation thinking about the healing process and the laying on of hands ceremony, he changed his mind. What if nothing happened? Would he make a fool of himself? He decided that he loved God and that God was the one who could heal and not the minister standing at the altar.

In those few moments before the healing service began, he prayed to Jesus, "I have always loved you, Jesus. I adore you, Jesus. I believe that you, Jesus, have the power to heal if it is your will. I ask you now, with my heart and soul, to please heal my neck and take away this spur and awful pain. I am your faithful servant. I love and worship you. I pray faithfully every day."

Nothing happened to Gene that evening and he sat quietly while many people approached the altar to ask for healings during the ceremonies. He had faith that God would heal him when he felt comfortable to do so. At that moment he had a tremendous peace about the situation and felt in his heart that he was doing the right thing. Besides, what did that minister know about him? How could that minister have a closer relationship with the Father than he could? He pondered this philosophy all night and still felt peaceful about his decision.

The next morning when Gene woke up, he immediately realized that his pain had completely vanished. His neck moved easily back and forth and up and down as if he had never been ill. For thirty years Gene has remained free of pain and has been a compassionate and faithful servant of Jesus Christ.

He prays every day in thanksgiving for his miracle. Jesus showed him that it was possible to pray directly to him for favors. Gene was born a Catholic, but over the years he fell away from the Catholic church. But now as the years have passed and he has aged, he has returned to the Catholic Church because of his need to be more prayerful and devout to the Lord. He believes that, "all things work together for good for them that love God and to them who are called according to His purpose." (Romans: 8:28)

Gene Chodkiewicz
Gray, Georgia

Out of the Darkness Came the Dawn
∽⊙⊙∼

A lovely woman in her sixties, Marcella reached out to everyone with her warm smile and friendly open greeting. No one was a stranger to her. Because of her lovely, outgoing demeanor, no one would have ever guessed the secret she held deep inside her for fifty years.

From her early childhood into her teenage years, Marcella was emotionally and sexually abused by her father. He had his way with her whenever he wanted sex. For all the years she was growing up, she never felt free to have any friends over because she carried this secret with her wherever she went. It made her feel dirty and unworthy of anything. The guilt from this violation haunted her day and night. She couldn't get away from it. As far back as she could remember, her father was present in her life as an abuser. She has always questioned God about this and asked why she was never allowed to have a care-free childhood. But there wasn't an answer.

Marcella didn't think that her mother ever knew about the abuse. Her father said when her mother refused to have sex with him, it was now her duty. He repeatedly made her feel like a slut with his treatment. At the age of 17 she married her childhood sweetheart from their home town. She never told him about the abuse she suffered. Five years later she became pregnant with her daughter and hoped that this would be a joyous occasion. She thought that maybe for once in her life, she could live a normal, happy life.

Several months after her daughter was born, Marcella caught her father fondling the baby with her diapers down. When she saw this act, she was moved to rage. She refused to stand by and watch her child suffer the way she had all those years. She confronted her father saying, "That's the last time you will ever touch me or any of my children."

Marcella was afraid for her daughter whenever she saw her father. She didn't let her daughter out of her sight. She wanted to move away, but financially they weren't able to. Four long years later her husband obtained a new job in Dayton, Ohio. She worked at every type of job possible where she could to make ends meet. But she swore that her daughter would never suffer the way she had all those years.

Marcella didn't have an easy life after that. Her first husband died in his thirties from a heart attack. Her second husband suffered from Manic Depressive Illness and committed suicide in a terrible way. Her third husband was a loving man who worshiped the ground she walked on. But he also died an early death.

As a child of God, Marcella often wondered why she had to suffer the way she did. She carried her abuse with her wherever she went, day and night. This was something she never got over.

What happened to her as a child affected her for the rest of her life. When Marcella reached her sixties, she finally received therapy for this abuse. In a letter she confronted her father who was now dead. But this small action seemed to help her release all the anger, hurt, guilt, and grief over her traumatized childhood.

Ever since she left home as a teenager, Marcella was very devout and prayed every day for guidance from God, hoping for relief from her problem. She attended church and Sunday school regularly and volunteered for many activities. She has two lovely daughters, who supported and sustained her emotionally. She worked all her life, and no matter how destitute their situation became, her children never went hungry. They always received what they needed—a new dress for the prom, school supplies, a church trip. She worked full time in the office of the public school nearby and also baby-sat in the evenings for teachers and other single mothers. She was always helping people who were in need. In her spare time she crocheted dolls and sold these at local craft fairs. There were many days that she was depressed, but she reminded herself how lucky she was to be alive and picked herself up and went on.

In 1991 her children nominated her for the Miami Valley Mother of the Year Award sponsored by the Dayton Daily News in Dayton, Ohio. Her daughter Reita wrote:

From as far back as I can remember, my mother has been there for me. I was very young when my father died, but the void was filled by my mom. She made sure that whatever I needed, I had. She never let me know when money got tough, and we couldn't afford the birthday present or movie. She would baby-sit or scrimp on something she needed to see that I was taken care of.

She was always involved with my activities. She was president of the P.T.O., room mother, and the neighborhood "mom." When we went places, she made sure the neighborhood kids got to go, too. She was nicknamed the "Captain Kangaroo" of our neighborhood.

Now that I'm grown with kids of my own, she is still here supporting me in my bad times and laughing with me in my good times. She's not only the best mom, but also the best grandmother.

All my life she has been the most giving, caring, loving mother ever. She is the perfect mother of the year.

For many years Marcella worked in the office of the public elementary school and eventually retired from there. She always loved children and made a special effort to make them feel comfortable when dealing with problems. Several times during her career, she identified children who suffered sexual abuse and was instrumental in having them removed from the home and placing them in foster care.

When she discovered that we were looking for stories about miracles, she offered her life story to us as inspiration saying that it was a miracle that she lived through all she suffered and was still sane. She thanked God every day for a lifetime of help he sent her way. She was convinced that she was never alone. All the years that she was in pain allowed her to know the suffering of others and compelled her to try to help them get through it.

When Marcella saw the pictures from Conyers that we were going to use in the book, she said, "She had waited all her life to see evidence like this that Jesus was really here."

Only days after we received Marcella's story in the mail, we were told that she had been killed in a head-on collision. The accident happened after her story was placed in the mail, before we received it. She hoped that others might benefit from knowing that she survived and lived a good decent life with God's help despite all of her tragedies. "It is a miracle. It is a miracle," she said with conviction.

The Healing Power of Faith

In 1983 Suzanne received treatment for cancer in her left breast which resulted in a total radical mastectomy and several months of chemotherapy. The process was long and painful, but she hoped the treatment would conquer the disease. She felt she could endure anything as long as it brought a cure in the end. Her daughter was only thirteen at the time, and Suzanne didn't want to miss out on her adolescent years or miss seeing her unborn grandchildren grow up.

Fortunately, Suzanne was free of cancer until 1986, when another growth was found in her right breast. Much to her dismay this one was also malignant. Suzanne suffered through another radical mastectomy followed by another course of extensive chemotherapy. She accepted this treatment with courage and faith that the medication would kill all the cancer and she could return to a normal life. They removed all her lymph nodes too and now the veins in her arms were terribly damaged compromising the circulation. Some days both arms became painfully swollen and difficult to use.

Not long after she had received the treatment for her breast cancer, on a routine chest x-ray, the doctor discovered fluid in the plural cavity and a suspicious area on the lower third of the lung. When this area was biopsied, the results diagnosed one of the fastest growing cancers of the lung, oat cell. The several gallons of fluid taken from the pleural cavity that day also carried malignant cells that confirmed the diagnosis.

Gravely, the doctor gave Suzanne her death sentence. "At the most, you have only two to three weeks to live. The CAT scan has shown us where the cancer has spread."

Suzanne was so stunned by the terrible news that the full impact of it didn't sink in until late that night. She realized that she would have only a few weeks of good life, if that, before the end. Her daughter was still young, sixteen, and she didn't know what was going to happen to her.

She opened her Bible and prayed desperately to Jesus for help: "Please heal me, if this is your will. I want to stay here and take care of my daughter."

As she skimmed through Bible verse after Bible verse hoping to find some comfort for the devastation she felt, the words "you are healed" jumped right out at her in such a way that she knew immediately Jesus had healed her and answered her prayers.

The next day when she returned to the doctor, he checked her all over and suggested another x-ray. Much to his amazement, the films were clear. There was no evidence of cancer. Even after all these years, Suzanne's cancer has never returned.

Ever since that day she has become a very devout Christian and prays to the Lord every day in thanksgiving for her life. She knows that she wouldn't be here without this miracle. She now has three grandchildren and more on the way. She loves them so much and helps her daughter raise them in every way she can. She attends their little league games, and keeps them in the evening when her daughter works. Every day is a wonderful gift from God and she wants to give this to her grandchildren with her love.

Suzanne Smith

The Death Angel

Since her healing, Suzanne has seen many spiritual visions and been introduced to what she calls out-of-body experiences. Late at night before she falls asleep, angels come for her and take her back to heaven for a short period of time. She feels as if these visits renew her spirit and fill her soul with love and peace; then the angels return her to her life here on earth and leave her safe and sound in her bed.

One night as she was about to fall asleep, the death angel came for her just as the others did. She sensed he was the death angel immediately because he was tall and dark. She wasn't afraid of him because his soft, peaceful, and pleasant demeanor made her feel as if he was an angel of God. She felt as if she knew him, as if she had seen him before.

They flew down a tunnel—he was on his horse and she was flying behind him. They flew to Washington D. C., the capital of the country. Before they reached the city, however, they saw a huge black cloud hanging ominously overhead. The angel reached down and lifted the dome from the capitol, exposing the senators inside who were arguing during a heated senate debate. The men were visibly angry and yelling at each other with vindictive expressions on their faces. In an instant, the men turned into serpents who began to writhe and coil around each other. Without warning, their giant mouths opened and they consumed each other in their wickedness.

The death angel rose up into the sky, put the top back on the capitol, and told Suzanne that the people were going to lose everything if they didn't pray for peace.

Suzanne Smith

A Community of Love

For many years Janice served as a food service supervisor for a Georgia prison. One morning when she was getting ready to go to work, she didn't feel quite well. But she just shrugged it off and continued dressing. When she walked into the bathroom, she collapsed on the floor. Even after weeks of tests, the doctors didn't know the cause of her problem. Some days she could manage little tasks, but on other days, she couldn't get out of bed. For her this debilitating condition was abnormal and turned her life up-side-down. She had always been perfectly healthy, and now she depended on friends and family for everything.

In 1991 she suffered a severe shock when the doctor finally told her the diagnosis was multiple sclerosis. Afterward, she spent five and one-half months in bed. She tried all the usual drugs for this disease but had little success. Eventually, she was able to manage daily necessities by using a wheelchair. She was a single woman, and for the first time in her life she had to depend on friends for help.

Janice suffered for five and one-half years as a wheelchair-bound invalid. But in 1998 the people and churches of Eatonton, Georgia, rallied together to help and to pray for Janice. For many days the people in Eatonton prayed for her recovery. During that time she woke up one morning with more energy than she had felt for several years. Soon she had gained enough strength to stand alone, to support her own weight. Within a week she began to use a walker. A few days later she was able to walk with the support of only a cane. Now she is walking and doing most things without any aid and without any medication. Looking at her, a stranger would think she was the picture of health.

After a complete physical examination, Janice received an astounding clean bill of health from her family physician. The specialists also confirmed that Janice is in remission.

She attributes her renewed good health to a miracle from God as a result of all the prayers sent up to heaven for her by the community of Eatonton, Georgia. She prays every day in thanksgiving for the miracle of healing that she knows came from the Holy Spirit. Janice's return to good health is not only a wonderful gift from God but also an instant gratification to all the people of the community who prayed for her.

Many other people have been personally touched by this miracle, too, and in some cases, those who were lukewarm in their faith now believe that the Father, Son, and Holy Spirit are active in their lives. Janice's illness and need for prayer brought all the churches together, too, in a effort for one cause.

"For where two or three people are gathered together in my name, there I am in the midst of them." (Matthew 18:20)

Janice Campbell

A Lay Renewal Mission Trip
eᴏ⑥ᴏᴗ

"Everyone has a miracle story," said Bill. "I have my share, and they seem to stick to me like ticks. No matter how hard I try, I can't get rid of them. When I reach that unexpected tough bend in the road, they come out like Jehovah and speak to me at that blackest moment. They say, `The Lord is still with you. He has never left you. Call on him.'"

About twenty years ago Bill and other members of his Presbyterian church set out on a Lay Renewal Mission Trip to Florence, South Carolina, with anticipation and love in their hearts. He eagerly looked forward to this gathering of religious families from all over the South. It was a time of rejoicing in the Lord and of personal spiritual growth. Families from all over were housed by the parishioners of a small town church and enjoyed the hospitality of their spiritual food and their physical nourishment.

Several ministers came too. Bill and the others spent the days listening to sermons so powerful they thought the dead could be raised. All had a chance to take turns at the pulpit, if they felt so called. The rest of the visitors spent the days with heads bent in fervent prayer and the nights singing floor-stomping hymns. It was a time of spiritual growth and many souls were saved. It was a glory to behold.

Some of the women were great cooks, too, Bill recalled, and the tables were laid with Southern delicacies of every type, just for their enjoyment. He can still remember Mrs. Dunn's strawberry pie or Nellie May's broccoli casserole. Barbecue and fried chicken were always main course staples.

After a few days Bill and his friends grew to feel like family members of the parishioners they visited and knew of their family tragedies and celebrations. Bill stayed with a family whose husband had recently suffered debilitating pain in the heel of his foot. The doctors had diagnosed a bone spur which crippled him. He had lost time from work and had no other means of support. He was afraid to take the several weeks off needed for surgery for fear that he would lose his job. At dinner that first night, the family and invited guests prayed to the Lord for healing. His whole lifestyle was at stake. But nothing happened. That night they went to the prayer services, and everyone there continued to pray for him.

Bill will never forget seeing the relief and awe on the man's face the next morning when he prayed in thanksgiving to the Lord. All the pain this man suffered in his heel completely disappeared. Tears of joy streamed down his face as he thanked the Lord for his gift of healing. Even after all these years Bill has not forgotten this experience.

Bill Neely
Milledgeville, Georgia

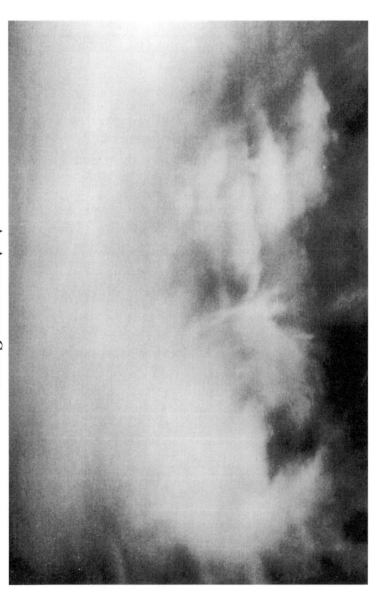

An Angel in the Clouds

Photo by Betty Davis

The Greatest Gift
⊷⊙⊶

When Betty Davis was only ten years old, she knew that her life mission was to work with the mentally retarded. When a young mentally retarded girl who lived in her neighborhood was taunted and teased by the other children, Betty befriended her and felt from the beginning that she knew just how to communicate with the girl. When the other children were afraid of the child, Betty invited her over to play paper dolls. Betty was never uncomfortable around her, and realized then that she wanted to spend her life working with the mentally handicapped. She knew in her heart this work was something she was supposed to do.

Betty's dream was realized when she became a social worker and began her days as an agent for the developmentally disabled. She worked at several different residential centers before she found a position at one in Apalachicola, Florida. While scanning her client's files one day, she realized that the young retarded girl who had grown up in her neighborhood and who inspired her to go into this kind of work was living at this residential center. Her life had come full circle; this woman was in her care again.

"It's funny how life works," she said, "I never expected this to happen."

While Betty was on an airplane flight from Syracuse, New York, to Atlanta, Georgia, she looked out the window at the beautiful cloud formations. The view was so compelling that she pulled out her camera and snapped a picture. She became lost in the clouds' unusual shapes and enjoyed her otherwise boring flight. During that time she remembered the days that she worked at the centers and how her life had progressed. She also reminisced about her four children. In the hustle and bustle of continuing her travel to Tallahassee, Florida, she forgot all about taking the picture of the clouds out of the airplane window.

Several weeks later she took her film in to be developed. When she picked up her pictures, several of the technicians were discussing her photographs. One said, "We just love the image you took of the angel." At first she didn't know what they were talking about.

When she saw the photograph, she remembered that she took only a photo of the clouds and the unusual formation. She admitted that she never saw the angel. She also admitted that she didn't know how it appeared on the film. She had always taken photos of the supernatural and collected pictures of ghosts, but it never occurred to her that she could catch the image of an angel on film. The technicians suggested that it was a supernatural phenomenon, a gift from God. She wondered if maybe this image was a gift to her for all the years she spent helping the disadvantaged because she was thinking about her clients when she snapped the photo. Or maybe it was just a gift.

This is not the end of the story. When I was signing books in Vienna, Georgia, a woman came up to me and told me her story about an angel. She said a friend of hers snapped a picture out of the airplane window, and when the photograph was developed, an angel appeared in the picture. I asked her if she could get the photo for me, and she did. It was a lovely likeness of an angel wearing a beige gown with a blue ribbon tied around the waist. The gathered dress ended in a simple ruffle around the edge of the hem and looked so real that one would never think the image was supernatural. A bright supernatural light obliterated the facial features. But the lovely beige wings resembling peacock feathers in design were so clear each tiny curve and eye at the end was visible. The entire background on the photo was brownish-black.

The woman who took the pictures said that she saw sparkles of light outside of the window that were so lovely she snapped the photo. I asked the lady if I could use the photo in this book, but she said she didn't know who took the picture originally. It had been passed around from friend to friend to friend. Several months elapsed and still the owner of the photo could not be located. I was disappointed because I thought that many more people could benefit from the story if they saw it in my book.

The time neared for me to stop collecting stories, and I still hadn't heard from the woman about the angel. I thought that either she didn't want to give me permission, or she still couldn't find the owner. I don't like to push people because many times they withdraw their stories in the end if they are hesitant. So I bemoaned the loss of the airplane story, and let it go at that.

The weekend before I sent the manuscript to the printer, I met Betty, and she told me about the photo she took out of the airplane window. At first I thought she was the owner of the photo from Vienna. But after talking with her, I realized that her picture was another image. She sent me her picture, and it is the one seen here on the first page of the story. The silhouette of an angel in the cloud formation.

One evening I was visiting with a friend in Atlanta, and when he heard about the angel picture taken from the window of the airplane, he was surprised. Then he told me another story of another picture taken from the window of an airplane. He said that the owner didn't see the angel either, but the face, wings and upper body were clearly visible. It was a wonderful photograph where the wings faded into the clouds behind.

It seems as if angels are appearing to us all. We never know where they will turn up next. I just know that from now on, I will be looking out of the airplane window for that once-in-a-life-time chance that I might see an angel.

Crossing the River with Jesus
ఴఄ

Oscar Mincey fought a long and difficult battle against lung cancer before he died. Because he was a career military man, his reputation of strength, integrity, and honesty was of prime importance to him during his life. In the final hours before his death, he never wavered from these qualities and displayed the same deep courage that he drew on all his life, a courage that came from his deep faith in God. He followed all the doctor's directions, took the prescribed medications, and was never confused or delirious. The following account from Oscar's wife Nancy describes the unusual events that occurred before Oscar died. She believes that all his visions during those painful hours were real and extremely inspirational for them both.

On August 8, 1997, Oscar and his wife, Nancy, were watching the television in their bedroom when Oscar nodded toward the end of the bed and smiled.

Nancy asked him who was there, and he answered, "There is a lady standing at the foot of the bed, and she has the saddest expression on her face that I have ever seen."

"Do you know her?" Nancy asked.

"No, I don't."

Oscar's visions never frightened Nancy; she knew that the "Lady" was an angel sent from God to help him cross over to the other side.

Oscar started to cry. "Please Jesus, take one more. Take Nancy with me."

Oscar and Nancy were lying on the bed holding hands, and Oscar became quiet for a few seconds. Then he turned to Nancy and said, "Baby, I looked at you, and you were bathed in the most beautiful light, but Jesus pushed you out of the light and said, 'She can't go. It's not her time yet. She has much to do.'"

Nancy never doubted anything Oscar said because of his military background. He was always so exact, and to the point.

A few moments later, Oscar became very frightened and said, "Baby, when I held out my hands to Jesus, the spirits from the other world tried to take me away, but the lady would not let them."

When Oscar was afraid during these last days, the "Lady" would comfort him. She talked to him in ways that Nancy couldn't. And at other times he talked with Jesus. Oscar told Nancy that Jesus did come across the river to get you when you died, just as he had been taught.

One night the "Lady" told Oscar that he would "disengage" in the morning. Nancy asked Oscar what disengage meant and he said that he didn't know. Oscar asked the "Lady" when he was going to die, and she said that she didn't know the exact time.

Nancy tried to take his vital signs because she is a nurse and she was wondering about his condition. Oscar refused to let her saying, "Baby don't do that to me. You don't understand. I just got word. They said it's my time to go."

Nancy wondered if he thought she was trying to put an IV in his arm at that time, and he didn't want her to do it, because he pulled his arm away.

Later that day Oscar was talking to Nancy when he told her that Jesus was coming for him in a boat.

For some reason he started to cry, "Don't go. Don't go. Please don't tell me that I have missed my last chance."

Nancy tried to comfort him and told him that Jesus would give him another chance. Often when Nancy tried to comfort him, she couldn't. But then he would tell her that the "Lady" was there with him, and he would seem comforted.

On several occasions Oscar looked up at the ceiling and said, "That is the most beautiful light I have ever seen."

Nancy never saw anything—but the love and peace that she felt in that room and still feels today is the most powerful feeling she has ever witnessed.

Oscar died at 5:10 am on Wednesday, August 13. At 4:00 am Nancy awoke, and Oscar was already dying. He was flailing his arms about, and he was afraid. He was shoving things away from him. Nancy hugged and kissed him and told him how much she loved him and how much God loved him. She read passages out of a prayer book to him, and he became more peaceful. Finally, his eyes closed and she called to him and told him she loved him. He opened his eyes and looked at her three more times before he died.

⤜◎◎⤏

On bad days when Nancy is upset, needs to be comforted, and is thinking about Oscar, a strange thing happens, she smells the aroma of his after shave lotion and knows his spirit is nearby.

On another occasion when Nancy was alone and feeling very sad and crying, she spoke out loud saying, "Oscar if you are near, please let me know."

She sat in the bedroom for a few more minutes and nothing happened. When she walked down the hall to the kitchen, she heard the sounds of music coming from her bedroom. She didn't remember leaving any music playing, so she went back to see what was causing the noise. When she reached her dresser, her music box was playing "The Way We Were."

The drawer to the music box had been pulled out to start the music playing, but she hadn't pulled out the drawer or wound up the music box. She knew then that Oscar's spirit must have activated the music box. It had to have been him, because she was the only person in the house at the time.

Nancy Mincy
Midway, Georgia

Strawberry Daiquiris
ల౦అ

It was Christmas vacation, and crowds of frantic shoppers packed the stores and grabbed up merchandise of every size and type. "A tie for Uncle George . . . perfume for Aunt Minnie. . . ." The requests were endless. Hot pink and gold foil wrapped boxes stacked in displays symbolized the priceless tokens to be given as the rare gifts of the Magi. Elaborately festooned Christmas trees shimmered and glittered under the bright lights. All around, excitement and merriment electrified the air.

Hope and her friends dashed from one store to another in a mad effort to find the perfect gift before the three o'clock movie. Weary and hungry from their shopping spree, the girls slipped into Applebees Restaurant for a quick bite to eat before the matinee. The place was empty, and the girls breathed a sigh of relief in hopes that they would be served quickly.

When the waiter placed a platter of nachos and cheese in the center of the table, everyone dug into the huge mound of sour cream, tomatoes, and lettuce in the center, not missing the bits of hot peppers. Hope recalled happily, "My mother always loved hot peppers on everything she ate, and so do I."

The girls helped themselves to the appetizer, not saying a word in reply. Almost two years before, Hope's mother had died of cancer after a lengthy illness. The girls knew that Hope missed her mother even more during the holidays. They tried not to mention it and tried in every way to cheer her up. The main course came quickly, too, and the cute waiter buzzed from one girl to the next asking, "Is there anything else? Do you need more tea? How about desert?"

"No, we're fine," said Meghan.

"We are in a hurry to get to the movie," answered Bonnie. Everyone began eating as fast as they could.

When the plates emptied and the pleasant feeling of fullness set in, the conversation picked up.

"What are you getting for Christmas, Meghan?" Hope asked teasingly, "Forty compact discs." Everyone laughed.

"Well, a few might be nice, but not forty. I am hoping for a new stereo. My old compact disc player is broken, and I would love a new one. What are you getting, Hope?"

"I don't know. My father has given me some money and told me to get what I want. But," she sighed deeply, "I really want a camera."

"Well, maybe you'll get one. Your dad is going to get you more than that," Meghan replied.

At that moment the waiter stood quietly at the end of the table, sheepishly clearing his throat. He glanced from one girl to the other as a smile danced across his face, "I was wondering if you girls would like a Strawberry Daiquiri."

"What . . . er . . . a . . . we don't drink yet," answered Meghan, as she sat up straighter and ran her hand through her hair.

"No, I don't think fourteen is old enough yet," said Bonnie, laughing.

"No, this is without alcohol," the waiter interrupted. "I made too much for an order and have lots left over. It would be . . . a . . . a gift."

"A gift. Sure, we'll have some."

"A gift. Yes, I'll have some too," answered Bonnie.

"No, I don't want any," answered Hope, a strange expression crossing-her face. She looked as if she were forcing back tears. "No, I don't want any."

"Oh, come on Hope. It's just a little for Christmas. What's

the matter? Haven't you ever had a Daiquiri before?"

Hope didn't say a thing for a few seconds, but finally relented, "I guess I'll try one."

"That's the spirit," the waiter said as he disappeared into the bar.

"Wasn't that the strangest thing? I have never had anything like that happen to me before," said Bonnie.

"Imagine, a waiter giving us a free drink. I bet he is trying to flirt with us," said Meghan.

"Well, you can try to enjoy it. I know I will," said Bonnie.

The Daiquiris were presented in large styrofoam cups.For some reason Hope didn't want hers and set it down hard on the table. "I don't know what you're making all the fuss about. My mother always made me strawberry daiquiris. Whenever she got a drink, she made me one without the alcohol. That's all she ever made me to drink. Not cokes or ginger ale, we always had strawberry daiquiris. It was our treat. Always . . . always."

Every one was so surprised at Hope's response that they didn't know what to say. But later they all wondered if Hope's mother's spirit had been there with her that day in the restaurant. She gave her daughter the most precious gift for Christmas, a sign that she was there watching over Hope and guiding her. The strawberry daiquiris were a special treat that only Hope could fully appreciate.

Musical Serenade
ℰⴰⵔⴰⵌ

In the summer of 1996 my daughter, Meghan, had just turned thirteen. She and her friends were calling boys and trying to be adults. I was racing behind them, making sure they stayed out of trouble. Our phone was constantly busy as they called each other just to see what was happening.

The girls came over to my house for a sleep over and stayed for three days. They played tunes on our antique grand piano until I thought I would scream, but I was thankful that they were happy to be under my roof, where I could keep an eye on them. They pounded out the notes to Beethoven's "Für Elise" and acted as if they had heard it a million times. At first they hit only the first two or three notes but several hours later were able to play the first stanza. I kept asking them why they were playing this classical piece. They always answered that they didn't know. But before long, I thought I knew why this music was haunting them.

By the second day of the piano playing, I became more suspicious. I knew my daughter had not learned this piece in her piano lessons; and when I asked her where she had first heard it, she said that Jennifer must have learned it from her boyfriend.

When I asked Jennifer why she played the piece, she answered, "I don't know. The notes just keep going through my head, and I can't do anything else but try to sound out this music."

When I told Jennifer's mother about the music, she too was surprised and added, "Jennifer never goes near our piano. And she has never had piano lesions either."

By the third day of a constant sounding out of a rather difficult piece, I knew, without a doubt, what was going on. My mother had died the February before. In her last few years of life we weren't very close because her husband and I didn't get along. I never had a chance to say good-bye to her.

My mother played the piano for years and graduated from the Peabody School of Music in Baltimore, Maryland. She possessed a musical gift and often played popular pieces by ear. All my life, whenever she sat down at the piano to play, her warm up exercises began with the music of Beethoven, and the first score was "Für Elise." She never sat down without starting with "Für Elise." To my mother, this music was as familiar as "Chopsticks."

By the third day of the girls' playing the same music, I knew that my mother's spirit was inspiring them to play. I don't know why. Maybe it was a sign to me that her spirit was there. Maybe she was trying to help her granddaughter and her friends. I'll never know the real answer. All I know for sure is that this was not a coincidence. Her spirit was influencing their behavior. They didn't understand why they were playing the music over and over again either. But I did. And with every note, familiar memories of my mother returned. From the moment I heard the first few notes the girls played, I thought of her.

Even now, three years later, whenever these girls get together, they gather at the piano and play the same lovely music. Now it comes naturally, and they can play the entire first score. I wonder if my mother's spirit is nearby.

An Angel Near Death
∽୶ৎৣ৶৵

In 1992, Kim was scheduled for out-patient surgery and a exploratory laparotomy for pain she had been suffering in her abdomen. The doctor assured her that this was a routine procedure without risk. She met with the anesthesiologist several days before the surgery to sign an operation consent form, and have her blood drawn. The lines on the form suggesting the possibility of hemorrhage, stroke, and even death from the anesthesia upset her. Agreeing that she understood that these problems might occur and taking the responsibility away from the doctor upset her too. But the anesthesiologist only waved away her worries, saying that these incidents happened only once in a million operations and signing the form was routine for every patient.

She had asked a few family members and a friend to accompany her just to give her moral support, and they were happy to do so. Kim and her family arrived at the Medical College of Georgia in Augusta at 6:30 a.m. that Thursday morning. The nurse tried in vain to start the intravenous fluids without success. Finally, she gave up and called the same anesthesiologist. He wasn't concerned, and without too much difficulty he was able to start the fluids running. He reassured Kim again that there was only a one in a million chance that anything could go wrong and she would be through by lunch.

The anesthesiologist was right and nothing unusual happened to her then. Her doctor completed the surgery by noon and she was back home in Milledgeville by 3:00 p.m. Her two young daughters spent the night with her sister so they wouldn't get upset seeing their mother after surgery. A close friend stayed with her overnight to help her with any problems that might come up.

By 3:00 or 4:00 a.m. she awakened feeling very hot and suffering terrible pain all over her abdomen. Her friend was leaving for work around 6:00 a.m., but she begged him to stay. He assured her that the pain would go away soon. He thought the pain medication had just worn off and suggested that she call him if she needed anything. By 7:00 a.m. she was doubled over with pain. She didn't know what to do, so she called her sister who was able to come around 8:00 a.m. to take her back to Augusta to the doctor's office. By 9:30 a.m. she arrived at the office and was still experiencing excrutiating pain, to such an extent that she could barely stand up. The office secretary was not moved to sympathy and just told her to wait in the waiting room. They called her back to have her blood drawn and when they had finished, they asked her to have a seat back in the waiting room. Kim and her sister waited until 11:00 a.m. when the doctor finally saw her. Based on her blood work and the terrible pain she was experiencing he decided to admit her to the hospital. By that time though, she was curled up into a fetal position from the pain and couldn't even straighten up. When he tried to examine her, she couldn't stretch out on the examining table. No one had given her any pain medication. When she reached the hospital, her temperature was 105 degrees. The pain continued to be so severe she could hardly stand it. She was finally admitted to the hospital at 4:30 p.m. that afternoon. The nurse put a stomach tube down into her esophagus because her stomach had blown up the size of a watermelon.

Her condition worsened by the minute. Everything that came out of her stomach was either brown or black. She was probably hemorrhaging, but the doctor couldn't find out where it was coming from. Perhaps the doctor nicked the bowel while exploring her abdomen. No one knew for sure what caused the terrible problem.

The doctors said that all they could do was go back into

surgery. They performed many x-rays and found nothing wrong. The blood tests were showing that her white blood count was 12,000, which was very high and suggested an infection or peritonitis. All she knew was that they said her red blood count was very low. By this time she was passing in and out of consciousness. She heard that they couldn't get her fever to break. Her sister had gone home and was taking care of her children. Her friend was sitting by her side.

She remembers a nurse on the late night shift with long brown hair and a Irish accent coming in talking to her and praying aloud for her whenever she could. A certain intern came in often, too, to check on her. She didn't know if a doctor came in or not. She remembers seeing her friend sitting at her side and watching her sleep.

The following Wednesday, seven days after her surgery, the medical team told the family that there was nothing more they could do for her. She remembers the conversation although she still suffered excruciating pain all over her swollen abdomen. They continued to give her pain medication and antibiotics. She remembers waving good-bye to her friend.

Kim was exhausted and still in a semi-conscious state. Everything went black, and she felt as if she were moving. Soon she felt she was speeding as fast as a train through a tunnel. She saw the frames of her life passing by, scenes framed like pictures, which were as clear as if they were happening then and she could distinguish every image and knew who the people were. It was as if her life was passing before her. Soon she saw a tiny light the size of a pin hole in the distance, which eventually became larger and brighter. Without warning, she came to a screeching halt and felt her body jump from the impact.

As soon as her body stopped, she felt as if she was being lifted up and cradled in someone's arms. She knew that her grandfather was there and she felt as if she were a baby again, small and frail. She sensed the presence of gentle beings, but couldn't see them. She felt no fear and remembers the profound peace that she had never experienced before. The further she progressed into the light, the more peace she felt.

She remembers a heavenly aroma and a music that transcended any she had ever heard before. When the brilliant light completely engulfed her, she was overcome by extreme peace and an all-consuming, powerfully compelling love. She has never forgotten that feeling. But all she could think of were her two young daughters. If she went with the light, they would be left without their mother. The whole time she was away, she was thinking about who would raise her angels.

She looked around and felt a large, strong hand grasp her shoulder. There were no verbal messages, only the feeling of complete love and peace. The hand turned her around and gave her a huge shove back down the tunnel. On the way back she sensed the presence of souls around her, but couldn't see any of them. They were of all different ages, from small children to older ones and yet, mysteriously all the same age. She knew this without question but didn't know how. They were nudging her forward as she passed back over to the other side.

When she awoke, she was in her hospital bed. The nurse was there and mentioned that she had been in a sound sleep, a stronger and deeper sleep than she had slept since she had been there. The doctors took more blood.

Kim remembers her doctor and three other doctors coming into her room. They were accompanied by the hematologist and other lab personnel. Kim saw the shocked expressions on their faces.

"All your blood work has returned to normal and we don't know what happened. Only hours ago we had lost all hope for you. You should have died." The doctor scratched his head. "We never diagnosed the problem. Maybe there was a pin hole rupture in your intestine and the antibiotics have taken effect. We don't know what the answer is."

From that moment on she healed, although still in a weakened state, by Friday she was released from the hospital. But the message that she has felt ever since and still feels today is to teach and relay to others the experience of unconditional love, to those who upset her deeply, even to her enemies. Before the moment of her near death experience, she didn't know what unconditional love meant.

In the years since her near death experience, Kim has grown spiritually and feels the presence of the Holy Spirit guiding her in every phase of her life. At some moments she has even experienced the gift of healing to help others emotionally and physically. Sometimes she can even predict the future for herself and others. Every day is a new learning experience for her on her spiritual journey of growth. But the most important element from her near death experience and being in the presence of God was the lesson she learned of unconditional love and forgiveness. This has been a very difficult exercise for her because she suffered a very painful and traumatic divorce from her husband. But after resolving her grief and anger, she has gained a tremendous internal peace. She now feels free to move on to experience the blessings of the rest of her life.

Kim
Milledgeville, Georgia

MAP OF LOURDES

MFH Graphics

THE STATUE AT THE GROTTO

The Miracles at Lourdes
౿౷౿

Every year over two million people visit the Grotto at
Lourdes, France, to show their devotion to the Blessed Mother,
Our Lady of Lourdes, and Saint Bernadette for the healing powers of Jesus Christ which flow through the waters in a natural
spring. Many of the visitors are looking for miracle cures for
their illnesses or for answers to their prayers. Ever since a fourteen-year-old visionary named Bernadette Soubirous first saw
the image of The Lady in the cleft of a rock and dug into the earth
near the Gave River, many visitors who have touched the spring
waters have witnessed miraculous cures. In 1933 Bernadette
Soubirous was canonized Saint Bernadette, and the Grotto of
Missabielle is now the greatest center of pilgrimage in the Ro-
man Catholic world.

On February 11, 1858, Bernadette, her sister Mary, and
friend Jeanne Abadie went to the Gave River to gather some wood
to warm their homes. Their families were poor, living in the worst
conditions in the Cachot, a part of the old prison in the Rue des
Petits Fosses, in Lourdes. The long, bitter winter had created a
scarcity in firewood, increasing the price and causing a grim ad-
versity for those of little means. Mary and Jeanne took off their
shoes and crossed a shallow spot in the riverbed to an island beyond, hoping to gather some larger pieces there. The location
was near a cliff known as the Massabielle rocks and a Grotto
which was naturally formed inside the mass of stone and resembled a cave.

When Bernadette came along, she didn't want to take off
her stockings and wade through the freezing water because she

suffered from acute asthma and was afraid she would get sick. She threw several big stones into the narrow stream to make a path, but was never able to collect enough pebbles to raise the path over the level of the water. Finally, she knelt down to take off her stockings. At that moment she heard a great clap of thunder. She stopped what she was doing to look around, but seeing nothing, she continued stripping off her stockings. She heard the thunder again and stood up to try to discover the origin of the loud noise. A wild briar bush nearby was being blown fiercely by the wind and rattled loudly against the stones. At that instant a golden cloud arose from an opening in the rock where the bush flapped. In a heavenly light, a Lady appeared above the bush in the cleft of the rocks, that formed the Grotto.

The following quotes are excerpts from the book *Lourdes: A History of Its Apparitions and Cures* by George Bertrin, Kegan Paul, Trench, Trubner & Co. Ltd, London.

"She was young and beautiful," said Bernadette, "more beautiful than anyone I had ever seen. She looked and smiled at me, and made me a sign to come forward without fear. And, indeed, I was no longer afraid."

Bernadette took out her rosary beads and began to pray. The "Lady" also prayed her rosary along with Bernadette. When the rosary was over, the heavenly brightness which preceded her trailed behind when she vanished within the rock.

Later, Bernadette described the Lady as resembling a young girl of sixteen or seventeen: "She wears a white dress; round her waist is a blue ribbon which falls the length of the dress almost to the ground. Her hair can hardly be seen for a white veil which falls behind, over her shoulders, and below the waist. On her naked feet are golden colored satin rosettes. In her right hand she holds a rosary with white beads and a golden chain which glitters like the rosettes on her feet."

While Bernadette was praying in the Grotto, Mary and Jeanne returned from gathering firewood. Thinking it an odd time to pray, they teased Bernadette. But the fourteen-year-old just ignored them. She asked if they saw anything unusual, but they said no.

Later that evening during prayers, Bernadette began to cry. When her mother asked what the problem was, Bernadette confessed what she had seen that day at the Grotto.

Her mother was so disturbed by what she heard that she scolded the child and warned her not to return to the grotto. She thought the child was imagining these things.

Finally, four days later, on February 14th, the children returned to the spot, and the lady appeared again, just as she would sixteen more times.

This time several more of the village children accompanied Bernadette. The second she reached the bush, she knelt down to pray and immediately shouted with joy, "She is there! She is there!"

The other children brought Holy water and quickly gave it to Bernadette who threw the water at the apparition and stood back, afraid she had made her angry. If the vision had been an evil spirit, the Holy Water would have sent it away.

Bernadette said to the children, "She isn't angry. On the contrary, she is smiling."

The children saw a luminous light coming from Bernadette's face, and the transformation frightened them so much they began to cry. They called her name, but she was "transfixed" as she watched the niche behind the bush.

At that moment a neighbor woman came by and tried to get Bernadette's attention, but the child was in a trance. She appeared to be in ecstasy. The neighbor left immediately and summoned her son. When the son arrived, he was overcome by the spectacle of the child's face as she worshipped the apparition. Never before had he witnessed such a vision. The child's face had been transformed; she was so lovely, serene, and even mystical that he could hardly believe his eyes.

When Bernadette's mother came to fetch the child, she was so angry that she was about to beat Bernadette. But the neighbor woman stopped her, saying, "How can you strike such an innocent child? She has done nothing wrong. I have never seen such an angel. To me she looks like an angel from heaven."

Mme. Soubirous didn't beat Bernadette, but she did keep her away from the Grotto for three more days. By February 18th, several of the village ladies had persuaded Mme. Soubirous to allow Bernadette to return to the Grotto; only this time she went very early in the morning.

The group had just reached the Grotto when Bernadette called out, "She is coming. She is coming." This time the child brought a piece of paper and held it out to the apparition, politely asking her to write down her messages.

"It is not necessary for me to write down what I have to say to you," The Lady said before asking Bernadette to return for a fortnight. Then she said, "I promise to make you happy, not in this world, but in the next."

Each of the following fourteen days, Bernadette returned with her mother, and after word of each day's vision spread, the crowd of people accompanying the child grew until there were literally hundreds of spectators.

On the 20th of February a Dr. Dozous was among the people who represented almost the entire village of Lourdes. He wanted to examine the child and didn't believe the stories about the visions. He thought the child abnormal in some way. The following is his account, which is an excerpt from the book *Lourdes: A History of Its Apparitions and Cures*.

"As soon as Bernadette was before the Grotto she knelt down, took her rosary out of pocket and began to tell her beads. Soon her face altered, a fact which was remarked by all those near her and which indicated that she was seeing the apparition. Whilst with the left hand she told her beads, in the right she held a burning candle, which was frequently blown out by a strong breeze coming from the River Gave. Each time this happened she passed the candle to someone close at hand to re-light.

"I followed Bernadette's movements very attentively, so as to be able to study her completely, from several points of view, and at this precise moment I wanted to know the state of her circulation and respiration. I took hold of her arm and placed my fingers on the radial artery. The pulse was quiet and regular, the breathing easy. There was nothing to indicate that nervous over-excitement might be reacting on the organism in a special way. As soon as I let go of her arm, Bernadette moved higher up towards the Grotto. I noticed that her face, which until then had looked perfectly happy, began to wear an expression of sadness. Two great tears fell from her eyes and coursed down her cheeks. This change had surprised me and when she had finished her prayers, and the mysterious being had disappeared, I asked her what had been taking place and she replied:

"The Lady for an instant did not look at me, but looked beyond my head and then again at me. I asked her what made her sad and she said: `Pray for poor sinners; pray for the world which is in such trouble.' I was quickly reassured by the kind and peaceful expression on her face, and just then she disappeared."

"When leaving the spot," Dr. Dozous added, "Bernadette retired modestly and simply without paying attention to the public's focus of which she was the object."

Bernadette continued to visit the Grotto every day accompanied by hundreds of people. On the seventh visit the Holy Virgin gave her three secrets and made her promise not to reveal these to anyone. She never did.

On February 24 the crowd watched as Bernadette dug for the source of the Holy Healing Waters of Lourdes. During her ecstacy and vision trance, while in the middle of saying the rosary, Bernadette got up as if she were listening to directions and moved closer to the Grotto. In a special spot she knelt down to the ground and began digging in the sand with her delicate fingers. Before she dug, the earth was completely dry. As she continued to dig, water rose up into a little puddle, creating a muddy hole. She cupped her hand and drew a palm full of water up to her mouth and drank of it. When she had finished, her hands and face were covered with muddy sand.

The spectators didn't understand this change of behavior. Some thought Bernadette had gone crazy, and they left, angry that they had come at all. Others knelt down and took some of the mud and water home with them. Later she told the onlookers that the Lady directed her: "Go and drink at the spring and wash in it."

Dr. Dozous reported: "I found that it was dry everywhere except where Bernadette had hollowed a little hole with her hands where the spring immediately flowed."

By the next day the spring had thickened to a constant flow of pure water the size of an arm, and by the following day it had grown to a large quick flowing stream. It was reported in 1908 that the spring gave out 122,000 liters of water in twenty-four hours. Another report in 1970 stated that the spring gave out 9000 gallons a day. This flow has continued since that moment in 1858 when the child first scratched the ground. The people who carried home the first samples of water and mud returned very excited and reported that miraculous healings had occurred to those who touched the water and earth. Ever since, hundreds have visited the spring looking for healing and have received it.

On Saturday, February 27, the Lady appeared again and gave Bernadette the message: "Go tell the priests to build me a chapel here."

March 4th was the last day of the fortnight, and by the end of the eighteen visions, as many as twenty thousand people attended the viewing. The Lady came again to Bernadette, and the ecstasy on her simple face lasted more than an hour. The people were content to witness the angel-like expression on Bernadette's face during the Lady's presence. They never saw the Lady themselves.

Miracle cures continued, and in July 1858 a Mgr. Laurence appointed a commission composed of sixteen members to investigate the nature and origin of Bernadette's visions. Doctors were summoned to testify that each eye witness interviewed was of sound mind.

On January 18, 1862, the commission gave the following report, which is excerpted from the book *Lourdes: A History of Its Apparitions and Cures*.

"We declare that the Immaculate Mary, Mother of God, really appeared to Bernadette Soubirous on February 11th, 1858, and on following days as often as eighteen times, in the Grotto of Massabielle, near the town of Lourdes; that these apparitions have all the characteristics of truth and that the faithful are justified in believing them to be true. We humbly submit our decision to the judgment of the Sovereign Pontiff, who governs the Universal Church."

Bernadette attended the convent school that now bears her name: the Hospice of the Sisters of Charity. Even though she was besieged with serious asthma attacks, she applied for entrance into the nunnery. In 1866 she was accepted, even with her frequent illnesses, and she lived at the mother house of the Hospice in the Convent of Saint Gildard in Nevers, 300 miles away on the

Loire River. Throughout Bernadette's life she was questioned by every authority possible, the Bishops of the Church, the Mayor of the town, and even representatives from the King of France. Her mental health was examined, and although doctors devised hundreds of questions to trip up the young woman, she held fast to her story. Even on her death bed, December 12, 1878, twenty years after she saw the first apparition, she confessed to a delegation of Catholic Bishops that the visions were of the Virgin, The Immaculate Heart. Even though hundreds of visitors to Lourdes claimed many miraculous cures, Bernadette still suffered from severe asthma, tuberculosis of the lung, and she died a long, painful death from a tuberculosis tumor of the right knee. She received the last Sacraments three times. The miraculous cures were not meant for her, however, but as a visible sign to others that the Holy Spirit is alive and well.

Bernadette was buried at Saint Gildard, and pilgrims visiting her grave have also confessed to receiving many cures from their illnesses. In 1925 Bernadette's body was exhumed for the third time to be examined by the priests for her canonization. Her body was not in the least decayed although it had never received any of the preserving chemicals used in the embalming process. This was truly an unusual occurrence because the bodies buried in 1879 were usually completely decomposed over time. Her skin was still intact, only the eyes were slightly sunken. Her body had taken on a dark bluish color because of the previous openings of the coffin and exposure to the air. Her body was bathed and wrapped in a shroud leaving the hands and face exposed. These were covered by a very thin layer of fine wax hand crafted by specialists of the day. She was then enshrined for all to see and is on display today inside a gold and glass coffin in the Convent of Saint-Gildard, in the city of Nevers. On December 8, 1933, Bernadette was canonized by the Pope.

In 1883, the twenty-fifth anniversary of the apparition was celebrated, and the first stone of the Church of the Holy Rosary was laid. Six years later the same church was opened and consecrated with a splendid ceremony.

THE PRESERVED BODY OF BERNADETTE

MFH Graphics

The Cures

Religious sites generate strong emotional reactions, and many times people believe spontaneous healings are from the powers of God when they are not. Because doctors believe the body can sometimes heal itself from strong mental powers, the spontaneous healings that began when people touched the Grotto springs at Lourdes were questioned. Many of the healings appeared to be authentic, but skeptics still wanted to believe that hysteria was the main reason so many miracles occurred at the same location. Many people are reluctant to believe in miracles at all because they seem to go against nature. The miracles at Lourdes have risen above all the skeptics' reasoning, and the testimonies of those healed have been the proof that spontaneous healing is possible and does, indeed, happen.

Even though the authorities at Lourdes asked for a certificate from a licensed doctor as well as other witnesses' reports, they still wanted more proof. In 1882 a Medical office was started. Pilgrims to Lourdes brought with them certificates from their local physicians stating their illnesses, cures tested, and length of their illnesses. Even their personalities were examined, the cure recorded and further data documenting the absence of disease collected several years later.

All insignificant cases were put aside; the others were open for examination by anyone who was interested. Believers and skeptics alike were allowed to examine the records. The medical charts were filed, published, and are still available to the public.

Dr. Henry Head stayed at Lourdes for a number of years and examined the ill when they arrived, gave them numbers, evaluated them during their stays and before their departures. His accounts are in the book *Lourdes: A History of Its Apparitions and Cures* by George Bertrin.

In his records he wrote about a boy of eleven. The boy looked perfectly normal to the doctor, and his mother agreed that he was a normal healthy boy. But she confessed to the doctor that in 1900 when the boy was seven, he came to Lourdes with terrible spinal deformities. He was unable to walk or stand on his own. His only mode of transportation was crawling on his hands and knees. But when he left Lourdes, he could stand up, walk on his two feet, and even run like a normal seven-year-old.

Another case was of a thirteen-year-old girl who had come to Lourdes as a deaf and dumb child, was cured, and returned several years later to pay tribute to Our Lady of Lourdes.

Many different kinds of diseases were cured, and their reports were taken from the Annals of Our Lady of Lourdes in the Medical Registration Office. By 1908 the office had registered over 3,350 cures, and if they had added those which had not been officially recorded, the number would have totaled over 7,000. Every known malady, from cardiac disease, tuberculosis, brain afflictions, pleurisy, bone afflictions, joint infections, tumors, skin diseases, cancer, rheumatism, blindness, deafness— all forms of deformities and diseases—were instantly cured when the visitor bathed in the spring waters at the Grotto. Yet, many went away disappointed and remained in the same condition. No one knew who would be cured and who wouldn't.

One young girl, Lea Courtout, with an incurable spinal disease—Pott's Disease, which caused an S curvature of the spine and protruding humps in both her back and front—dreamed of going to Lourdes and saved every penny for the trip. But she donated all her savings to help her parents' desperate need to pay their overdue rent. When the money went, she lost any chance she ever had of going to Lourdes. But the following year, her goodness was rewarded. In 1895 she was admitted to the National Pilgrimage and allowed to go free of charge.

When Lea arrived, she had a certificate from her doctor identifying her disease and the remedies that had been unsuccessful. On August 21, she bathed in the piscina, and a few days later, her doctor wrote:

"After examining Miss Lea Courtout, I beg to state that:

(1) The spine is quite straight.

(2) There exists a slight protuberance of the two final dorsal vertebrae.

(3) The left shoulder is slightly raised and the right side of the chest is a little thinner than the left."

In a word, save for these insignificant traces, the evil had disappeared in a few seconds. The spine which had been crooked for months, had suddenly become straight."

The doctor who attended Leonie Charltron was overcome by the miraculous cure of his patient. On July 21, 1869, she suddenly regained her health in the piscina. Spinal curvature disappeared, and the doctor, Gagniard of Avallon, had the honesty to write:

"The sudden instantaneous cure of Miss L. Charltron at Lourdes is certainly miraculous and absolutely authentic. You may defy the most learned, the most experienced, or the best physician to explain the instantaneous cure of Miss Charltron who was wasting away in the last stages of paralysis and fever, with suppuration of six vertebrae. The case was beyond treatment, and it is impossible to quote a similar cure within the realms of science."

E Gagniard, Senior M.D.

In 1896 fourteen patients came to Lourdes with advanced and chronic tuberculosis from the hospital Villepinte. Eight were cured, and six returned home unchanged. Three years later the eight who had been cured remained cured, and of the six not cured, two remained very ill and four had died. In 1897 a larger party came to Lourdes from Villepinte, twenty patients in all. Among those, eight were cured either completely or partially, and the others eventually died of the disease.

In 1897 Villepinte sent an even larger party of patients, twenty-four, suffering with advanced tuberculosis. These patients were very encouraged and hopeful by the success of the others, but still in the depths of despair in their suffering. Upon their return, eight of the patients were completely cured, six experienced relapses, and ten were unchanged in their illness and eventually passed away.

"If contrary to all expectation they were stopped on their hasty road to death, it cannot be attributed to any other influence than the intervention of God, the Master and Author of Nature. In a few moments the bruised and emaciated lungs were healed. They regained their normal state, and life returned to bodies exhausted and devoured by fever.

"In a few months, sometimes even in a few weeks, these lucky girls grew healthy and stout, recovering as much as 10, 20, 30 pounds of flesh. 'It was like a resurrection,' said one of the nuns who nursed them." *Lourdes: A History of Apparitions and Cures.*

"Aurelie Bruneau, of Chabris (Indre), was born deaf and dumb. At the age of twenty she put a few drops of Lourdes water into her ear on three successive days, and, on October 11, 1872, she suddenly found she could hear and speak. Of course, she had to learn her words, for language is not acquired intuitively. The family doctor, De la Mardelle, who examined her after the event, wrote as follows:

'From earliest infancy, this young girl who was placed under my care, offered every symptom of natal deaf-mutism. On October 11th, on her return from a pilgrimage to Lourdes, she instantaneously recovered the faculty of hearing. The cure was certain and undeniable. The deaf and dumb girl can hear and speak.'"

A declaration was made by MMe. Paul Lallier, the woman who bathed Clementine, and who actually witnessed her miracle.

"On Friday, August 21, 1891," wrote Madame Lallier, "I was at Lourdes, in the children's piscina, helping to bathe the patients, with Mille. Cornet of Paris, and several other ladies who were strangers to me. I had already bathed several children in the miraculous water when I saw Clementine Trouve coming towards me. I can remember perfectly well the impression she made on me, as I was struck by her innocent appearance and her pale and sickly face. She walked with difficulty leaning on a heavy stick.

"I cannot exactly remember what became of the bandages which had bound Clementine's foot, and which had been taken off before she was handed over to me; I believe that she had them in her hand, and that in the excitement of the cure they were dropped into the water, from which they were afterwards taken.

"Having said the 'Hail, Mary,' I began the prayer, `Blessed be the holy and Immaculate Conception,' but I could not finish it, for suddenly the little patient jumped up, crying out, `Let me go—I am cured!'

"And she was cured indeed by the miraculous water of Our Lady of Lourdes. At this very moment I saw on her right heel a large scar which closed, so to speak, under my very eyes. The flesh rejoined and seemed to be reuniting itself. I could not believe what I saw. Delirious with joy, she wanted to go at once to the Grotto to thank Our Lady and to leave her stick. I was so upset that I couldn't follow her; my legs refused to carry me.

A few minutes later, however, I joined my little protegee,

who walked without the slightest difficulty, and I took her to the Medical Office, where there were several doctors."

Five million religious pilgrims still visit Lourdes every year and hundreds of miracles still occur. A hospital has been built on the site to accommodate those too sick to visit for the day. Visitors who claim healings still register their illnesses, and recoveries at the "Bureau Medical de Notre Dame de Lourdes" (formerly the "Bureau de Constatations") which has been given the task of proceeding with all the necessary examinations. It receives each year more than 2,000 doctors of all nationalities, upon whose demand, whatever their beliefs, the office gives free access to all their records. Its works are supervised by an international medical committee.

Some people think that the location of the spring waters in the Grotto is the most Holy Spot in the Catholic Church. Over 5000 cases of reported healings have been documented and approved. But whatever the reason, the mere mention of the word Lourdes conjures up inspirational visions of healings and testimonies to the power of the Holy Spirit.

Bibliography

Bertrin, George. *Lourdes: A History of Its Apparitions and Cures.* London, England. Kegan Paul, Trench, Trubner & Co. Ltd., 1908.

Cavendish, Richard, Editor. "Lourdes," *Man, Myth & Magic: An Illustrated Encyclopedia of the Supernatural.* New York, New York. Marshall Cavendish Corporation, 1970, p. 1650-1653.

Personal Gifts from the Holy Spirit
❧◎◎◞

I have experienced several miracles in my life that opened my eyes to the power of God and the existence of the supernatural. These were not great miracles, but small indications from God that I was not alone in this vast, lonely world. The first occurred in 1974 when my mentally handicapped five-year-old daughter, Jennifer, was dying in Johns Hopkins Hospital. She had been a patient there for almost three months while the doctors were trying to find out why her condition had deteriorated so fast. She suffered with a rare hereditary disease known as Hurlers Syndrome. In this disease the enzyme that metabolizes fat is missing and the by-product is deposited in the tissues and bones eventually causing mental retardation, physical deformities, dull vision, deafness and finally death in early childhood. She was suffering from the symptoms of hydrocephalus, water on the brain, and the doctors finally decided that the bones in her brain stem where the spinal fluid is fed to the brain had become too deformed to do their job and the fluid built up causing increased pressure in the brain.

Jennifer was scheduled for a brain arteriogram at 7:00 a.m. in the morning. I went to the hospital early to see her before the procedure. My husband refused to go because he was angry that the doctors had kept her in the hospital so long. He didn't see any need for it. He wanted her to be left alone and didn't believe that any of their diagnostic studies were necessary or helping her condition. My parents had deserted me years before because they couldn't face her illness. My husband's parents were available, but not for this kind of support. My seventy-four-year-old grandmother was the only one who helped us out, and she was caring for my two-year-old son while I was at the hospital. So I walked down the cold, empty hallway of the pediatric unit completely alone and felt an overwhelming sense of impending tragedy. I had no idea how I was going to get through the next few months with this dying child that I loved so much. I had never felt that low or that abandoned in my life. Suddenly, as I walked down the hall, I felt the pressure of a hand squeeze my shoulder. It was large, strong and reassuring. The hand was so strong that I felt the warmth of it go through my whole body. When I turned around to see who was there, I was shocked to see no one. The hallway was completely deserted. But the feeling of pressure and warmth was still there on my shoulder. It felt like an oasis in the middle of a desert. Was I imagining this? Was I losing my mind? For years afterward, I asked these questions, but in my soul, I've always known that someone else was there with me. Perhaps it was my angel, perhaps it was Jesus; all I know is that it was there when I needed someone.

My feelings of foreboding and tragedy were realized that morning. Jennifer must have felt them, too, because when the nurses pulled her stretcher onto the elevator, she raised her hand in a final good-bye. Jennifer arrested when they were trying to give her the anesthesia. The tube they were placing down her throat stimulated her vagus nerve which caused her heart to stop. She died seven days later after not being able to regain an adequate heart rate. I'll never forget that long, terrible week. But most of all, I'll never forget feeling that strong hand on my shoulder and the power it has had over my life ever since that day.

My husband and I suffered deeply as we tried to regain hold of our lives in the face of our grief over losing Jennifer. He seemed to find comfort in drinking alcohol, and I found comfort in searching for God and trying to find some meaning for my grief. We experienced many low points and just tried to get through one day at a time. We often wondered why that tragedy had happened to us. All of our friends had normal, healthy children. They even had loving families to give them emotional support when they needed help. We never found the answers to any of these questions. But we were given support in other ways. On several occasions just as we turned out the lights in our bedroom at night, we heard the sound of wings fluttering around the room. When we turned on the light, we never saw a stray bird or bug or bat or anything flying. But when the light was turned off again, the flapping of wings continued. After a few nights we began to believe that the sound of wings flying overhead was coming from Jennifer's spirit, her angel wings. Even now, twenty-five years later, when I hear the sound of wings, I know her spirit is near.

After Jennifer's death my husband and I had a difficult time emotionally. It seemed to us that when Jennifer died she took with her all the love we had ever felt for each other. We were dead emotionally. The only feelings we had left were for our three-year-old son, Andrew. One night after an intense argument, when a long, cold, silence permeated the room, we both heard voices singing; a beautiful choir of voices broke into our hostile silence. We listened intently, and my husband commented on it first. "What's that? It sounds like angels singing. Do you hear that?"

I heard the music from thousands of etherial voices that I had never heard before, but I was so angry at him that I denied ever hearing anything. I remember thinking at the time that there must be a heaven. I left the room without saying another word. After that our marriage continued to disintegrate, and we were finally divorced. But neither he nor I will ever forget the experiences we had during Jennifer's life, her wonderful gift of love and her angel wings afterward.

After my divorce I worked as a registered nurse for five years doing private duty nursing in ten hospitals in Baltimore, Maryland. The nursing registry sent me to all the hospitals in town, and many times I would arrive at work at 6:30 a.m. to find a patient on a respirator, newly discharged from the intensive care unit. I stayed with the patients until their conditions improved or, as in many cases, until they died.

On several occasions during that time, patients whom the doctors predicted would die soon became better and even went home. I'll never forget taking care of a nineteen-year-old boy who had been injured in an automobile accident. He was in a deep coma and had been for over a month. Because he could breathe only with the assistance of a respirator, the doctors considered him brain dead. The doctors said that it would be only a matter of time before his vital organs would shut down and he would die. His family never came in to see him because they had given up on him also.

From the first moment I took care of him, I was reminded of Jennifer. Seeing a young person in such a state hurt me. I knew the parents were going through hell, too. Each day I bathed him, changed his position, monitored the respirator and gave him his medications. During that time I often asked God why he would take such a young person. I simply couldn't understand it. But by the third day when I came to work, the boy seemed restless and moved his body from one side of the bed to the other. He opened his eyes and moved his face around, pulling against the tape holding the respirator mouthpiece in place. I decided to change the tape and wash his face. When I took off the wet tape, he spit out the mouth piece and breathed on his own. By that afternoon, he was shouting orders and speaking in confused phrases.

When the doctors made their rounds, they were amazed that

the boy had regained consciousness. They never expected him to because his brain studies showed massive damage, too much to sustain life. Immediately, they sent him to x-ray for further tests. By the end of the week, he was sitting up in the bed, talking to us, but he was still confused. At times he shouted obscenities to all of us. He seemed good at recalling all those words. But the doctors claimed that his recovery was a miracle because new tests showed that he was improved. They never understood what happened to him to bring him out of the coma.

⸎◎◎⸎

After being a single mother for five years, I fell in love and married my second husband, Jeff. We decided from the beginning to wait for several years before having children. After genetic testing, we discovered that together we could not transmit the genetic condition of Hurler's Syndrome. Both parents must carry the recessive trait in order for it to show up in the offspring. But I was still nervous and scared. Because I was in my late thirties, the doctors strongly suggested that I try not to have any more children. But I was stubborn and wanted one more child. I went to five different obstetricians, but only one agreed to take me as a patient. All the others refused, saying that trying again would be too much for me mentally and that they were not going to help me.

When I did finally become pregnant, I was terrified that something would happen to the baby. I had an amniocentesis to check out all the possible genetic problems. Since I was over thirty-five, this baby was subject to many other birth defects. One evening I became so afraid that something would happen to the baby that I cried all evening. It was almost midnight when I fell asleep and I dreamed that I woke from a deep sleep to the sound of a telephone ringing. I picked up the receiver and said, "Hello." The voice on the line was the voice of my grandmother who had passed away three years before.

She said, "Darling, don't worry. Everything's going to be all right."

I asked her repeatedly, "Where are you? Are you all right? What's it like to be dead?" She must have been surprised because she paused. Then her voice returned loud and clear. "Don't worry. Everything's going to be all right." She repeated her message several times and then vanished. I could hear the delight in her voice when I asked her about her death. But she never acknowledged my words; she only repeated her reassurances. It seemed as if she had been allowed to contact me only for this one purpose. I still miss her very much.

From that moment on, my anxieties evaporated. A few days later, we received word that all the tests were normal and that our baby was a girl. All of our friends and the people in our church had been praying for this little baby.

A few months later I had another dream that showed me the vision of a pretty young girl, all grown up, with red hair, and attending college. She walked along a tree lined sidewalk and placed her books down on the grass as she sat on the steps that led to an impressive two- or three-story brick building with white columns across the front. I knew immediately that this young woman was my baby. My dream told me that she was all right and not retarded and that she would live to be a college student. She would not die in infancy. How relieved I was. This vision carried me through a difficult pregnancy and all the years of her young life.

For the last two months of my pregnancy, I went into labor every night at midnight. Finally, the doctor put me into the hospital for two weeks to stop the contractions. When my baby girl was born, I was delighted to see her flaming red hair, just as I had pictured in my dream. She is truly a gift from God and has been a wonderful blessing to our family ever since.

∾∽☙☙∾

In 1985 I heard that my minister, Reverend Buchor, of the Brethren Church in Hanover, Pennsylvania, not far from our home, needed cardiac by-pass surgery. Many of the hospitals were performing this complicated surgery then, but when he remarked that his doctor said this surgery was as simple as a hernia, I was a little surprised. I knew from experience that it was more complicated than that. But I didn't say anything.

Several nights later, I woke up in a cold sweat, feeling terribly anxious for Reverend Buchor. I was getting a message that this operation was going to be the most difficult experience of his entire life, but that he would live through it and be all right in the end. I became overwhelmed with the burden of this message and felt compelled to tell him. How could I, a simple lady, tell the minister that he was about to endure a terrible and difficult surgery. I had no explanation for any of my feelings. But in my heart and soul I knew that I must tell him this message. One whole afternoon I cried and prayed about it. I became hysterical, because I didn't want to tell him. How could I give him such awful news? But I knew I had no choice, so I called him.

I said, "I don't know why I am giving you this message, but I feel compelled to do this. Your surgery is not going to be easy. In fact, it is going to be the most difficult experience you will ever have in your life. But the good news is that you will live through it. You will be all right."

His response was, "Oh, no. They tell me that this surgery is going to be very easy. You must be mistaken."

"I don't know why I am telling you this. But I know that I must. I have no other choice," I said, repeating my message. I was so upset that I started to cry and apologized for having to tell him this awful news.

Finally, he said that he heard me and he heard my message. I could hear a deep sigh after his words, and I knew I had upset him. I hated this, because he had been such a wonderful inspiration to me during my pregnancy. The last thing I ever wanted to do was to hurt him, and I knew that I had.

All during his surgery I prayed that all would go well. Later, I heard from his secretary that he was doing fine and in recovery. I was relieved, but I questioned why I had given him that message. Would he think I was crazy?

The next day I called the office to check on his recovery, and the secretary was very upset. She said that during the night he started to hemorrhage and that the doctors had to take him back to surgery. That was all she knew.

Weeks later, we were able to find out exactly what happened. During a sermon Reverend Buchor told the congregation about his experience. He remembered being in intensive care when all the buzzers went off; this time they were for him. The doctors gave him more medicine and said they had to go back to surgery. An artery had opened up, and he was hemorrhaging inside. Later that night he remembers regaining consciousness only to see the nurses working furiously around him. This went on for hours.

Through a fog of noise from the unit, he remembers hearing a voice say to him, "Through the power of Jesus you have been healed." After that he remembers falling into a deep sleep that carried him into the next morning.

Later that morning, the doctor came in to talk to him. He said, "You had a pretty rough night. I have to admit that I didn't think you would live. Your heart stopped, and we couldn't seem to get it going again. When it finally started, other things went wrong. Right now, I would say that you are living on a miracle."

Reverend Buchor told the doctor about the voice he heard and acknowledged that he, too, believed that he was alive because of a miracle from God.

It took Reverend Buchor a long time to recover. He spent many hours walking two miles a day to help his circulation. Telling his story to the church became an inspiration for everyone in the congregation. Many of these people had known him for years and believed his story.

It was hard for me to accept the knowledge that I had a premonition of his problems during surgery and told him about it. Maybe God wanted him to know this so he could prepare himself mentally for the experience and not give up. Whatever the reason, we had assurance that the angels were there with him all the time and that he would be all right in the end.

⋅⊙⊙⊙⋅

For eight years Jeff and I lived in Hanover, Pennsylvania, owned a farm and raised sheep as a hobby. Something inside me pushed me into the sheep business. It turned into a passion and we sold lambs, wool and even meat. We exhibited sheep at the Maryland and Pennsylvania Fairs.

Anyone who knows sheep knows that a sick lamb is a dead lamb. Baby lambs have a high mortality rate. Sometimes the mothers don't feed them and reject them. Other times the ewes have difficulty birthing their young. They suffer with every illness from bloat, pneumonia, scours, hoof and mouth disease, to parasites. Believe me, we experienced every one. But I became adept at saving frozen lambs born late at night in a frost covered pasture and deserted by the mother. I learned how to bring them back to life.

One year we decided to buy a calf, hoping to have her eat the meadow weeds that the sheep didn't eat. But the calf we bought was very sick from the beginning. She suffered with a bad case of scours and almost died. The veterinarian said she was allergic to the new spring grass and could eat only dried hay. Only after we had spent many hours at her side, rubbing her and talking her into living, did we wean her off the hay. As she grew stronger, she became very affectionate toward us and toward all the other animals. We named her Bethy the Cow. Many times I saw her mother the orphaned lambs and even let them nurse her udders.

My daughter, Meghan, was about three-years-old now and when I fed the animals every evening, she would stand in the middle of the hay stack and sing to them. She would sing her nursery rhymes and "Twinkle Twinkle Little Star". The animals loved this and would eat contentedly. One evening as Meghan was singing to the animals, Bethy the Cow began to moo to her music. She seemed to want to mimic Meghan's sounds. This gave me an idea.

Just for fun, every day at mealtime, Meghan and I decided to teach Bethy to sing. This was really just a joke, and I never thought that anything would happen. But every day we sang "Do Ray Me Fa So La Tee Do," just like the movie, *The Sound of Music*. We sang these notes very slowly, mooing to the tone of each note. Every time we saw Bethy we sang this song. Than we laughed and patted her head. She seemed to laugh, too, and mooed along with us.

When we told our friends and other farmer neighbors, they laughed at us and seemed to enjoy the little joke for Meghan's sake. One farmer confessed that he never even talked to his animals. I know they thought we were crazy. But we kept singing because this was fun for Meghan and it gave us something fun to do when we fed the animals every night.

At almost midnight one cool September night, when the full harvest moon was a large saucer on the horizon and when my husband and I were in bed turning out the light, we sat bolt upright in shock at the bellowing harmonious sounds of MOO, MOO, MOO, MOO, MOO, MOO, MOO, MOO. Bethy sang her song to the notes Do, Rae, Me, Fa, So, La, Tee, Do, baying at the moon, and never missed a beat. A cows baying at the full moon, can be heard for miles. The next day, our neighbor, whose house was at the top of the hill where our pasture ended, said he couldn't believe his ears. That night almost every neighbor within a mile had heard Bethy's serenade. But that wasn't the end. Every evening when it was time for dinner, she stood at the top of the hill and sang out her moos. It was amazing and in a sense a small miracle, even though she might have learned it easily because she was a smart cow.

Although this is not a real healing miracle, its implications have sustained me for many years. I always felt that if I could teach a cow to sing, I could do anything.

The following year we sold the farm, all the animals, and moved south to Atlanta, Georgia. The farm work had become more difficult for us and for our bodies, and we didn't want to spend the rest of our life doing that. We thought the move to a warmer climate and a closer proximity to our family would be a wonderful change. Still we were challenged in many different ways.

It didn't take us very long to sell the farm and buy a house in Atlanta. Unfortunately, the sales contract on the farm fell through, and when we purchased our Atlanta home, we needed a bridge loan. We were able to pay both mortgages for a little while, and thought we could sell the farm quickly. Our thinking could not have been more wrong. Months passed without our selling the farm. We depleted our savings, and I was forced to a full-time job. Finding one turned out to be more difficult than I ever dreamed. My nursing license had become inactive, and the only job I was eligible for was as a nurse on probation at the Veterans Hospital. The VA would accept me only on probation; otherwise, I would need to take a refresher course. The three-month course wouldn't be offered for two months. That meant I would have to wait for five long months before I could obtain an active license. I was stuck.

The first week I worked at the VA Hospital, I was over-whelmed by how sick the patients were and how dirty the hospital was. Because there were too many patients for the staff to provide adequate care, many patients went unfed and were generally neglected. I knew in my heart that I couldn't change any of these conditions. I was too small and powerless, whenever I made a criticism, the other nurses only stared at me in disbelief and laughed. I could see how over-worked and exhausted they were. Many of the nurses were injured from lifting heavy patients. They were given light duty, but more help was never sent by the administration. Every day we were short two or three nurses who called in sick. That left between twenty and thirty patients to be added to an already heavy load for the few nurses who came to work.

That first weekend I spent every hour praying to God for help. I had never prayed this long before in my life, but this seemed to be the only thing left to do. I was completely powerless. I knew what was good patient care with a large group, and I couldn't do it alone. Every day I worked, my integrity was compromised. Every day I remembered that if I could teach a cow to sing, I could do anything.

After a few days I saw small improvements. The rooms became cleaner because the hospital hired a new janitor for our floor. Some days I seemed to have superhuman energy and was able to get more work done. Then I noticed that patients who were expected to die, got better. Stroke patients became rehabilitated faster. One patient was admitted for a suicide attempt. He shot himself in his head and suffered severe brain damage. When I first took care of him, he was confused and immobilized with arm and leg restraints. His speech was incoherent, and he was incontinent. After bathing and dressing him, we lifted him up into the chair and immediately he began to talk clearly. By that afternoon, he was walking to the bathroom with help. The other nurses and doctors couldn't understand what was happening to these patients. It seemed as if they got well simply by my touch. In the morning they couldn't speak and by evening they were caring for themselves. I knew that the hand of God was at work there, but I didn't understand how or why. I simply treated the patients like people and gave them the respect they deserved, and they became healed in many ways. But there were always those people who never recovered and eventually died. I never knew who would get better or who wouldn't. I had absolutely no control in the matter. Sometimes I prayed extra hard for a patient, only to see him slowly pass away.

I had a deep faith in God, but my Methodist background didn't teach me about the power of the Holy Spirit. I never learned about the Pentecost and how the Holy Spirit could work miracles in my life and through my life. When I met a man I'll call Charlie, I reached a turning point as a Christian.

Charlie resembled the other patients on the seventh floor, scrawny, unshaven, slightly cyanotic and short of breath. But when I first met him, I learned immediately how different he was. He suffered from severe heart disease and was waiting for a heart transplant. The surgery would be performed by the surgeons from Emory Hospital and University Medical School. He had been a patient in the VA for two months already. If a heart came for him, he would have to be operated on within two hours or the heart would be too old. If he had remained at his home in Vydalia, Georgia, the distance was too far away to reach the hospital and prepare for surgery before the time expired on the heart. But he claimed that this was his last mission.

He said, "There are no coincidences. I have learned that much in my short life. God put me here just like he has put me in every other hospital I have ever been in." He glanced up and down the hall and motioned with his eyes toward the other patients sitting in the day room and continued, "I'm here for them."

Charlie said that he knew the Holy Spirit had been after him all the years he sold insurance to families all over Georgia. He saw a need in these people that never seemed to be fulfilled. This need was for spiritual guidance and enlightenment. This feeling gnawed him day and night until finally one evening, when he was lying on his couch watching television, the Holy Spirit knocked him on the floor and said, "I need your help."

He quit his job and traveled from hospital to hospital giving spiritual guidance to families in crisis. The hours were long and the work hard, and he claimed that it eventually broke his heart. Now in his last hours of life, he was living on the seventh floor of the hospital helping the poor, destitute men find God at the end of their lives. Charlie was the only one. No chaplin ever came up there. Once in a while a minister traveled from room to room and left a pamphlet on the bedside table. These men seldom took time to talk to the patients lying in the beds unable to reach the bedside table.

I had never heard anyone say that the Holy Spirit could knock a person on the floor. That image has stayed in my mind ever since. A week later when I was working in the ward, Charlie came in and said that he had been inspired to do something. He asked me if I minded if he prayed over me. I said, "No. I don't mind."

He put his hand on my forehead and prayed that the Holy Spirit would anoint me with his power and help. He said that he was giving me his mission because he was too sick to do it anymore. A few days later he came to tell me that the doctor was sending him home. The doctor said that his condition had improved so much that he was allowed to go home. That was the last time I saw Charlie, but I never forgot him.

After Charlie left, the chronically ill patients continued to improve rapidly. I had gained a reputation among the nurses, and they couldn't get over how the patients' condition changed. Sometimes they even joked about it. But when I pulled the muscles in my back several times, the doctor advised me that I needed to give up that heavy work or I would suffer with chronic back pain for the rest of my life.

Our farm finally sold, and we were getting back on our feet financially. With regret, I left the people who had become almost family to me and the patients who needed me so much. The working conditions never improved in the eight months that I worked at the VA hospital. But I was able to receive my Georgia Nursing license. Maybe I had been sent there for a lesson too.

In December, 1989, our family had lived in Atlanta for only nine months, and we were still trying to find a church. We had visited several in the area, but none seemed to meet our needs. One Sunday we attended the Duluth United Methodist Church, and right away it seemed to feel right. The people were friendly, and many new families were moving into the area. We had attended the church several times when my daughter and I went alone one Sunday. My husband was called back to work that morning and said he would see us later. During the service I kept wondering if this church was the one we should attend regularly.

When the service was over, I stopped to talk to several of the other parishioners, so by the time I reached the parking lot only two or three cars were left. As Meghan and I got into our automobile, I was still pondering whether or not we should join this church.

As I turned the key to the ignition, nothing happened. For some reason the key was frozen in the lock. Immediately a tremendous force overcame me, and I felt as if I was being pulled back into the church. The powerful pull was so strong, I couldn't move. All I could do was sit there. It was a centrifugal force like the one experienced in an amusement park when the ride is spinning. I could actually see it as a stream of energy that ran along the sidewalk. The shrubs behind the energy field were blurred and wavy. It resembled heavy ripples of heat. The force was pulling me into the church and I saw the ripples exit the church through the roof in the altar and choir area. I watched in disbelief as the ripples of energy bounced up and down on the roof resembling a musical pipe organ and continue up into the sky.

All I could say was, "OK Jesus. OK Lord. I am getting the message. I don't have to go into the church to know what you want."

The force lasted for what seemed like several minutes. A few more people left the church, and a man stuck his head out the front door to the sanctuary. When he didn't see anyone outside, he shut the door and locked it. I was still experiencing the force when the man came to the door.

At first I thought I must be going crazy. What was happening to me? My husband was a psychiatrist and I guess he was worried too. Afterwards, I still couldn't get the car started. The parking lot was deserted. Meghan and I walked around the back of the church to the office which was still open and used the phone. I told my husband I had car trouble and he needed to come get us. I was still shaking from head to toe from my experience. My hands trembled and my knees rattled together. Meghan and I returned to the car and tried to start it again. Nothing happened. Jeff arrived shortly afterward, and I saw immediately that he was upset. He motioned for me to move over, and without a second's pause the key turned and the engine engaged. I knew this wasn't my imagination. But we drove away and never had any problem with the car afterward.

We joined this church, and eventually I was able to speak to the minister about my experiences. But the car episode was only the beginning of my introduction to the power of the Holy Spirit. Already I was scared to death. No matter how hard I tried to explain away the things that happened at the VA, I couldn't explain these new experiences.

One morning not long after the church incident, I was sitting in my kitchen drinking my tea and reading the newspaper when I received another visit from the Holy Spirit. In an instant my large bay window was filled with a bright ball of light, and with this powerful light came an overwhelming sense of forgiveness and unconditional love. I was bathed in the light and was overcome by it. I had never felt such love in my whole life from anyone. It filled the kitchen. But it scared me again, and I kept wondering if I was experiencing this or dreaming this? Why is this happening to me? Am I special in some way? What is going on? No answer came.

The only time I had ever heard about the Holy Spirit was from Charlie, but now I had no one else to ask. I tried to find books about it, but they only repeated the verses in the Bible that referred to the Holy Spirit. In the Bible the Holy Spirit was responsible for anything happening, doors opening, windows into heaven, manna falling out of heaven, armies defeated, and people healed. Was the Holy Spirit after me? Was this the Holy Spirit? I started to pray to Jesus all the time, asking what I should do next. I was scared of my shadow. I kept thinking that I needed to go to church every Sunday and become a good member. I felt I had to change my life to fit His needs. I was a heavy smoker of cigarettes, 2 $1/2$ packs a day, and had tried to quit repeatedly, but couldn't. I thought that I must have a pure body to be acceptable by God. Then I brushed it off and told myself that He had chosen me and smoking was all right. Wrong!

I decided that my mission was to write a book about the VA Hospital and the men coming to terms with their spirituality on the seventh floor. So I began this task. One afternoon while I was writing, I had run out of cigarettes. I hadn't felt good all day and thought I was coming down with the flu. Suddenly, a huge white light filled the room, just like the one in the kitchen, and I again experienced this wonderful healing, loving power go right through me. Afterward, I was so tired that I got up and went into the bedroom to lie down. An hour later I awoke, just in time to wait for my daughter's school bus. I then needed to take her to her ballet class in Duluth. But a strange thing happened. I realized that I had lost my desire for smoking. I felt as if I had never smoked before. I emptied the ashtrays and wondered why anyone would use those things, although I remembered that I had smoked. On the way to the ballet class, I asked myself if I should buy some cigarettes just in case I might need one. At that moment I was passing the Duluth United Methodist Church, and I experienced that same centrifugal force pulling my desire for smoking away and pulling me into the church. That December, 1998, was the last time I ever thought about smoking. "OK. Lord. I'm getting the message." After the desire for smoking was taken away, my husband, who had wanted me to quit for years, began to take notice and realized that perhaps the Holy Spirit was working in our life. I was not hallucinating. The Holy Spirit was taking over my life.

All this attention was coming too fast, and I was overcome by it. I couldn't think of anything else, and I prayed when I got up in the morning, all day, when I was driving, and all evening. When I went to church one Sunday close to the time when I quit smoking, another extraordinary thing happened to me. As I was singing the hymn "Amazing Grace," my voice changed and my usually flat alto voice turned into a lovely, clear pitched soprano tone. It was the voice I had always envied and wanted. I had never been able to sing like that in my life. Eventually, I joined the choir and sang there every Sunday. At that point I never knew what was going to happen next. I had come to terms with the idea that I was not imagining these appearances by the Holy Spirit. It was time to speak to the minister.

Poor Harvey, I didn't envy his position here. As I sat in his office and explained what was happening to me, I told him how confused and scared I was by it all. He continued to shake his head up and down and say, "Un, Huh. Uh, Huh." He didn't seem to be in the least bit surprised. He didn't elaborate on what I said or try to explain it. He simply said, "Uh, Huh."

I tried to define the experience in the terms of "the force" in the movie *Star Wars*.

"I think the force is with me," I said.

He continued to shake his head. Finally, he said, "Yes, this sounds like the Holy Spirit. It sounds like the Holy Spirit is working in your life. It is quite a story. Keep me informed about the progress." Then he said, "Good-bye."

There I was, out in the cold again. Where should I go? Where should I turn? Whenever I spoke to anyone about the Holy Spirit they looked at me strangely. Soon I realized that people were trying to avoid me at any cost. I decided to keep the episodes to myself. I prayed about this, too. "There but for the Grace of God go I." I had no answers.

I met a woman who introduced me to the pentecostal church in her area and I attended the church for several services. People spoke in tongues. I told her about my experiences, and she wanted me to speak in tongues. I never did. But I thought my singing was a way to speak in tongues. When I spoke to her minister about what was happening to me, he said something peculiar to me. He said that they didn't allow any healing outside of the church. If I wanted to heal, I could come to their service. I was at my most vulnerable time, and I realized that everyone had his own ideas about the Holy Spirit. I finally told him that the Holy Spirit I knew worked alone and came to me only when He wanted to, not when I wanted him to. I was never able to call him up or use his power. It was not mine to use, but his to use through me. I had hit another dead end. When the minister spoke of healing limitations, I wondered how they healed anyone if they didn't go out to hospitals.

I embarked on a deep spiritual search. I wanted to know everything there was to know about the Holy Spirit and how he worked. In February I received a vision. Our church was arranging to set up a vacation Bible school in New Mexico that summer for the Navaho Indians at the Star Lake Mission. We were transporting 42 youths and parents and all the equipment to New Mexico to take care of us for one week. The vision I saw was of Jesus Christ standing in the desert in fire. I saw a blazing statue of Christ. I wrote this down in a letter and gave it to the ministers of our church. I said that this was my message to them. I knew I had to go. I felt that I would find the answers to my questions on the reservation in New Mexico from the missionaries.

Now I was seeing visions. Would it come true? Would the ministers think I was crazy? Only time would tell. I felt as insecure as I did when I told Rev. Buchor about his operation. I had to trust in God.

The Holy Spirit kept coming to me and finally, I asked it to stop for a while. Once when I was playing tennis, I fell and twisted my ankle. Within seconds, the Holy Spirit surrounded me with the cloud of wonderful love and healing. Within minutes the pain seemed to evaporate. My ankle wasn't completely healed, but I could walk on it. Just for a few minutes I wanted to be normal again, even though I was thankful for the healing touch.

Two months before the trip, my doctor suggested that I have a hysterectomy. When I spoke to the girls at church, one of them told me that this doctor wasn't a very good surgeon. He had caused other people she knew to have problems after the operations. After thinking it over, I canceled the surgery. Later I found out that this girl felt that she was compelled to give me the message about the doctor. I knew that it was from the Holy Spirit. When I scheduled surgery with another doctor, the rehabilitation time would be very close to the trip to New Mexico. I wondered if I needed the surgery at all. But I still experienced problems, so I went ahead with it.

Our trip to the Navaho Indian Reservation proved to be one of the most exciting experiences of my life. From the moment we arrived in Santa Fe, we enjoyed a tremendous sense of fellowship. We didn't know until the last minute whether we would be allowed to use the public school dormitory space at Star Lake Mission. Finally, with 42 people waiting in Santa Fe for word of where we were to sleep that night, the Navaho Tribal Council gave us permission. That was the beginning of the miracles that happened. I don't know what we would have done if they decided against having us stay there. In that short week we were able to understand how the Indians lived and what their days were like.

From the beginning the desert was unbearably hot, and the

constant wind sifted the sand into everything. A twenty-mile-an-hour breeze cooled our moist brows and teased our hair. We were always thirsty, and when we closed our mouths, we discovered grit between our teeth. Star Lake's living conditions were primitive, too, outside toilets, water hand pumped from a well, no air-conditioning in 98 degree heat, and no trees for shade. The small wooden chapel was the only building available for shelter and for teaching Bible School. We knew this ahead of time and brought tents and tarps to use as cover. But as soon as the men erected the tents, huge gusts of wind blew them down. The men finally gave up.

Early Monday morning they attempted to set up the tents again. The wind still blew, but as soon as the children began arriving, miraculously the wind died. Some classes met out in the open in the shade of the chapel; but if the wind had continued, all the papers would have blown away. As soon as the children climbed into the vans for their journey home, the wind began again, and the tarps and tents were ferociously blown down. It seemed to be another miracle. As soon as the children arrived every day, the wind stopped. Then, when they returned to the vans, the wind blew again in huge gusts, strong enough to tear down the tents.

On Tuesday night I was sitting in a pickup truck with the missionary who was telling me her experiences about the Holy Spirit. We hadn't been sitting there long when the wonderful feeling of love surrounded us. She oohed and aahed. Smiling in the ecstasy of His presence, she confirmed my impression that this was the Holy Spirit. We were both in prayer, absorbing the presence of the Holy Spirit when she shouted, "Look out the window!"

When I turned my head, I realized that the entire sky was red and striated like flames in a gorgeous sunset. The view from

Star Lake Mission, located on one of the highest hills around, extended across the floor of the desert for least 50 or 60 miles ending at the horizon. No town or house interrupted this panoramic view. In the center of the blazing red sky the pure white figure of Christ, with his arms outstretched, stood like a giant on the horizon. He wore a white toga, and the folds of the garment covering his arms resembled large fans. My breath caught in my throat, and I sobbed as I got out of the truck and stood there watching this miraculous sight as it slowly faded away. It was as if I had been struck dumb. I wanted to show the others who were inside the chapel for the evening service, but I couldn't move from the spot. The image was present for only two or three minutes. The only other person who saw the figure was the missionary. My vision had come true, although mine was of Christ in fire and the sky white. I was so awe stricken that I couldn't speak about it to anyone. When the minister came up later to verify what I had seen, I couldn't tell him. All I could do was stare at him as if I was in shock. Later I felt the Holy Spirit was keeping me from saying anything at all.

As one might imagine, with taking 42 men, women, and children into the desert, we had all sorts of emergencies. On Wednesday night we watched huge thunder clouds form and yield to the land a hard pelting rain, uncommon for that time of year. A four-year-old boy was injured when a heavy metal door from the chapel blew shut on his hand. Later the x-rays revealed the broken bone in his hand had already been perfectly set.

On the way back to the dormitory from the mission, the twenty-plus-year-old yellow school bus caught on fire. Thick, black smoke filled the cabin, and as twenty-some people were escaping through the back door, flames licked at the transmission and reached up through the floor. One of the men risked his life by smothering out the flames and turning off the full gas line.

The bus was only seconds from exploding. Fortunately, help soon arrived, and no one was hurt.

We were quickly learning about the poor and destitute conditions the Navaho struggled against daily. They traveled in broken down cars and lived in one-room houses without electricity or water. They trucked water from the nearest city and used their automobile batteries for their televisions. The tribe had been given money for these necessities by the American Government, but the tribal council used it for other things. Alcoholism, drug addiction, and their related diseases were high among the parents. The Death rate among teens is the highest in the country. The children attend boarding school all year, return home only for the weekends because the parents are too poor to provide transportation every day. The happy smiles on the faces of these children never divulged their secrets. To them we were laughingly described as "yellow hairs" and "gringoes." That they had no idea how deprived their circumstances were and this has haunted me ever since.

The last night we met on top of a plateau which was several hundred feet above the desert and overlooked the landscape for miles. There we ate a picnic dinner with all the leftovers from the week and celebrated the end of the trip with a prayer and worship service. A cool breeze gently soothed our tired muscles. As evening approached, the sky turned from turquoise blue to an awesome dusty pink. When the service was over, the minister prayed, saying that he hoped we had in some way helped these people and brought the word of Jesus to them. He shouted his words out over the precipice to the immense Navaho reservation and to God. He had hardly taken a breath when a huge silver comet soared across the pink heavens. It was as if God had shot a silver arrow across the firmament to show his appreciation for us. Yes, the Holy Spirit had been present the entire trip, and he was there at the end to give us his strength. No one on the trip has ever forgotten that moment.

Of course, someone in the church later said that it was probably just a piece of junk satellite falling out of the sky. But if this had been the case, the object picked the most perfect moment to fall. Sixty people had been picnicking on that precipice for several hours, and no one saw anything else fall from the sky.

I continued to relive the trip for months afterward. The power of the Holy Spirit had shaken my life beyond all imagination. I was still in shock when the clinic where my husband worked went out of business. We were forced to move to Milledgeville, the location of his current position. We prayed constantly that this was the right decision for our future. Only time would tell. I was terribly disappointed because I had found good friends in my writing group and had enrolled in the Disciple Bible Study Program at church. We were studying the Bible from cover to cover in two years.

Around that time we visited my family for the Christmas holidays. On the way home we stopped in Valdosta, Georgia, at its big shopping mall. I was waiting in the car for my husband, an unusual switch, when he returned with a page of the telephone book in his hand. I didn't know what he was talking about until he said, "I have found your father."

When I was three years old, my mother and father were divorced, and my grandmother retained custody of me. My father was forbidden to see me, and for my whole life I had never met him. I was now 45 years old. My step-father had adopted me, and he was the only father I had ever known.

"Here, go call him," my husband said. "He lives here in Valdosta."

I couldn't believe he was doing this. I had just visited my

adopted father, a good man who had raised me, and now he wanted me to call my real father. "Not today," I said. "Please, not today." I was afraid I would be rejected all over again. I had to think about this. My emotions had to catch up with my logic. As we drove home, my husband waved that page in my face. He never gave up. I knew this was meant to be.

Several days later, I called my father's phone number. I had no idea if this was the man or not. But he had the same name that my father did, and my mother always said his family lived in the small town of Valdosta, Georgia. A gruff voice answered.

"Hello," I said quietly. "Are you Ralph Bassford?" The person on the other side paused for a few seconds and finally answered, "Yes, I am."

"I don't know if you remember me, but this is Bonnie."

I'll never forget his words. "My God, you could have told me to sit down. How could you spring something like this on an old man without any warning. Yes, of course, I know who you are."

I suppose there are things in our life that no matter how old we become, we will never forget. One of these is our children. Even if we don't see them for forty-two years, we never forget them. This meeting was an act of God, because six months after I saw him for the first time since I was three-years-old, he died of lung cancer. He had been in Valdosta for only six months. He had lived most of his life in Seattle, Washington. When he returned to Valdosta for his mother's funeral, his family persuaded him to stay. He was destitute and an alcoholic gambler, but he was a tremendous story teller. I suppose I have inherited his ability to tell stories, although I can't tell them as dramatically as he could. After all those years, I began to understand who I really was. When I looked into his face, I saw mine.

Before we moved to Milledgeville, I took another job as a rehabilitation nurse at the Gwinnett Medical Center. We needed the money, and I worked the 3-11 p.m. shift. From the beginning "things" started to happen. The staff wasn't insisting that the patients work hard enough to develop their muscles. The rehabilitation process was slower than it should have been, and I could see where the problems were. I tried to encourage changes, but these were slow. Incredibly, some of the patients who were paralyzed from a stroke and couldn't talk, began to talk. One patient's right side was paralyzed and she couldn't speak. I was taking her pulse one evening, and suddenly a white light appeared over her wrist. When the light disappeared, her arm moved naturally. I never knew when a healing would happen.

I tried to pray over my father-in-law, but nothing happened. He had severe heart disease and eventually received a pacemaker. Sometimes, I wondered if the healings were my imagination, but they weren't. The Holy Spirit came when he wanted to, and it was always a surprise to me. I tried to pray over friends and others; many times no one was healed. I still pray, and sometimes the Holy Spirit grants us our wish.

Whenever I talked about praying and the Holy Spirit, I turned people off. They didn't understand His power and had trouble trusting in God. But after they experienced their own miracles, they understood. Unfortunately, even when people were healed, they had difficulty accepting that it was a miraculous intervention from God. So many try to explain the occurrence away, finding it difficult to believe that God will heal them.

I continued writing about the men on the seventh floor in the Veterans' Hospital. But I was not able to get the manuscript published. I decided that if people didn't believe in the Holy Spirit, then maybe they could believe in ghosts. After all the Holy Spirit was the Holy Ghost. Ghosts of Jesus were mentioned many times in the Bible before Pentecost. When I discovered that Milledgeville was home to many ante-bellum homes and buildings and these boasted about their benign resident ghosts, I decided to collect the stories in hopes of turning the full account into a book. So far I hadn't seen a ghost, but my experiences with the Holy Spirit prepared me for the worst, and I knew there was life after death. When I finally did see my first ghost, I read this passage about the gifts of the spirit: 1 Corinthians 12:10-11. "(8) For to one is given, by the Spirit, the word of wisdom; to another, the word of knowledge by the same Spirit; (9) To another, faith by the same Spirit; to another, the gifts of healing by the same Spirit; (10) To another, the working of miracles; to another, prophecy; to another, discerning of spirits; to another, various kinds of tongues; to another the interpretation of tongues. But all these worketh that one and the very same Spirit, dividing to every man severally as he will.

I have been given many gifts of the Spirit to use for His Glory when I need them. Over the years I have acquired the gifts of wisdom, knowledge, healing, miracles, prophecy, and now I see spirits. After interviewing many people who have seen ghosts, I realized that these experiences reinforced their beliefs in life after death and gave them deeper faith in God. These people have a sense of peace about them that others don't seem to have. They also see the spirits as having a sense of humor. It seems to me that the people who see spirits are the most gentle and kind people, and they live harmoniously with their spirits. I think that God has given these people the gift of seeing spirits, often called seers, because of their gentle, loving and accepting natures. Many others have seen spirits and even seen miracles, but they are too scientific in their thinking to believe their own eyes. I wrote my ghost books because I hoped that reading these stories would help others believe in life after death, the presence of good and evil, and the ultimate power of Jesus's Holy Spirit. I hoped that these stories would open people's awareness and belief system so that it was okay to talk about spirits. People see angels and other apparitions that are guides and helpmates. It is clear that Jesus is reaching out to each of us in personal ways only we can understand.

I tried to convince people that God was real and not a figurehead. I want people to know that God is there for us in our darkest moments as we walk down the lonely, deserted hospital corridor. He is there when we have lost all hope and sends His messengers to us in dreams. He moves obstacles out of our way that might keep us from His word. He sends his Spirit to intercede for us when we endure life threatening-surgery. He cleanses us from drugs, tobacco, and alcohol dependencies when we least expect it. He is there for us with the small decisions like what church to join. He is there with us when we face impossible trials and tribulations and sends His angels to guide us through our darkest valleys. He is there with the destitute in the most deserted areas of the world and sends our hands to help them. He heals us every day and protects us from harm. But He doesn't keep us from acquiring all the infirmities of the world. He has given us free will and considers our suffering a purification of our souls for the life that comes after this one. He never deserts us, and He is standing behind each and every one of us at this very moment, asking us to let him come into our lives.